The Friendship Book

A THOUGHT FOR EACH DAY | **2015**

The Friendship Book

*U*NBROKEN by time, or by distance,
  The chain of true friendship holds fast,
It's burnished by caring and sharing,
And stretches from present to past.

May always fond memories link us,
May always the chain bind each heart,
So though miles may keep us divided,
We never, from friends, truly part.

Margaret Ingall.

January

Thursday — **January 1**

NEW Year is a time for resolutions, a time for good wishes, a time for new beginnings. I think that these words sum up all that we could wish for each other on January 1:

All gloom be with the old year past
And this year be happier than the last.

May it be a happy and healthy twelve months for us all.

Friday — **January 2**

DO you remember when you were much younger, people would say, "An apple a day keeps the doctor away"?
I always had my doubts about that. But one thing I have always believed is that a smile a day can do a great deal of good.

It may not make us immune to germs and infections, but it certainly cheers both the giver and receiver.

You may be unfortunate and smile at someone who doesn't smile back. This can be very disconcerting! You are left wondering if that person has perhaps gone on their way thinking you are a little strange!

And perhaps they have. Or perhaps they are simply shy, or unused to such a warm gesture from a friendly stranger. Who knows, they might even try smiling at the next person they pass in the street!

So don't be downhearted. Yours, after all, might be the only smile that they receive that day.

Step out cheerfully and be generous with your smiles. I can promise you that you will certainly feel better – and so will everyone lucky enough to meet you that day!

W*HEN life has lost its pleasure*
And old delights depart,
They hold a secret treasure,
The buoyant young in heart.

When dark days bring rejection,
They turn their sight within,
And let sweet recollection
Its healing work begin.

They see the scenes of childhood,
When days were long and free,
The old path through the wild wood,
The flowering cherry tree.

They feel the sea breeze blowing,
They smell the scented air,
They see the great tides flowing
And know that God is there.

Such blessings they inherit,
Who seek a lasting truth,
And climb again, in spirit,
The mountain-tops of youth!
                                        Brenda G. Macrow.

D ID you ever skim stones across a stretch of water? Usually, when I tried, I would be too busy counting splashes to notice that the ripples just went on, and on, and on . . .

Mother Teresa may have had that in mind when she said, "I alone cannot change the world, but I can cast a stone across the water to create many ripples."

SITTING PRETTY

Monday — **January 5**

IF you use a computer for writing anything, or if you read a lot of e-mails, you will probably be familiar with the spell-check program that underlines in red any mis-spelled words. There's also a grammar checker that underlines in green any grammatically incorrect phrases.

Amazingly, I'm told you can also now get a program to check the tone of whatever you write! I suppose it must balance the number of positive expressions against negative words.

If only we could have a program like that for when we are talking to people! But we do. It's called our conscience, our sense of decency, or simply our love for each other.

Let's make sure it's installed and then turn it up for extra positivity!

Tuesday — **January 6**

CORRIE TEN BOOM was a Dutch Christian who lived through World War II. During that time, she lost several family members and experienced great sadness and hardship. Yet, rather than becoming bitter, Corrie realised that her life was a gift from God, and that she needed to share what she had learned.

At age fifty-three, she began a world-wide ministry which took her to more than 60 countries over the next 33 years. She testified to God's love, encouraging everyone she met.

Corrie wrote many books and spoke frequently in the post-war years about her experiences. Some of her most well-known books, such as "The Hiding Place" and "Tramp For The Lord", went on to become bestsellers, beloved by many. "The Hiding Place" was even made into a film in 1975, inspiring many to see God at work in life's most difficult circumstances.

Corrie always said, "If God sends us on stony paths, he provides strong shoes."

Wednesday — **January 7**

WE all enjoy talking to our friends and loved ones, either chatting over a cuppa or on the phone. But it's rather nice sometimes just to sit quietly and relax.

In this busy, noisy world, we all need a little silence now and then. Time to switch off and share some peace and quietness.

If we really know and understand the person we are with, then these words, by an unknown writer, will ring true: "Best friends listen to what you don't say."

I hope we can all do the same.

Thursday — **January 8**

IF the weather is dull today where you live, and you're feeling a little gloomy, consider this quote from inspirational writer Jim Beggs.

"Before you put on a frown, make absolutely sure there are no smiles available."

Friday — **January 9**

HANDS up all those who really look forward to their birthday. Well – not everyone does, and Carol was certainly one of that number.

"Then one year," she told me, "my little granddaughter insisted on bringing me a bunch of balloons. At first I felt rather foolish, but somehow her simple action made me realise that I should celebrate. Although I was a year older, I was also – hopefully – a year wiser. I had enjoyed another year of companionship with all my friends and, when I thought about it, I'd had more than my fair share of happy times. So ever since then, I have remembered those balloons and reminded myself to take proper pleasure in my day."

I do like that attitude. And may your birthday lift your spirits high!

Saturday — January 10

THERE is no doubt that social media has caught on in a big way, with Facebook being particularly popular.

A friend of mine posted this on her page the other day and I thought it was well worth sharing.

"You may not be able to go back and make a brand-new start, but you can start today and make a brand-new end!"

Sunday — January 11

PEOPLE might grumble about having to do the dishes or the household chores more often than they think is fair. But Brother Lawrence, a 17th-century Carmelite friar, spent every day either at prayer, in the kitchen or repairing other monks' sandals. His was the lowliest position in the monastery. And was he happy?

He described himself as "very well pleased with the post he was now in". But he would have been just as happy in any other position. Why? Because he delighted himself "in every condition by doing little things for the love of God".

Whether your lot is noble or lowly, if you take pleasure in the little things and in doing them for God then one thing is for sure – it will be a happy one!

Monday — January 12

WELL, here's a first! Francis Gay recommending war! It's not exactly as it sounds, of course. I'm simply passing on a New Year's resolution from the great inventor and statesman Benjamin Franklin.

"Be always at war with your vices," he wrote. "Be at peace with your neighbour and let each new year find you a better man."

It's a war worth fighting, a peace worth achieving and a goal for every man and woman!

TUMBLING DOWN

Tuesday — **January 13**

IN an arid desert on the west coast of Africa, the Namib beetle has found an inventive way of surviving. The beetle collects water droplets from the morning fog on its bumpy back, then lets the moisture roll down into its mouth, allowing it to drink in an area with no flowing water.

Shreerang Chhatre, an engineer and entrepreneur at MIT, wants to help the world's poor by refining what nature has developed. Chhatre works on fog harvesting, using a device that consists of a fence-like mesh panel which attracts droplets. The mesh panel is connected to receptacles into which the water drips. Thus villagers can collect clean water near to their homes rather than spending hours carrying water from distant wells or streams.

Nearly 900 million people worldwide live without safe drinking water, and although Chhatre agrees it won't be easy, he is working hard to change those statistics.

It is one of the beautiful compensations of this life that no man can sincerely try to help another without helping himself.

Ralph Waldo Emerson.

Wednesday — **January 14**

MOST of us will be familiar with the Serenity Prayer, which goes:

"God grant me the serenity to accept the things I cannot change,
Courage to change the things I can,
And the wisdom to know the difference."

But there's a more pro-active, if slightly tongue-in-cheek version, too.

"God grant me the serenity to accept people I cannot change,
The courage to change the one I can,
And the wisdom to know – it's me!"

Thursday — **January 15**

AN American mother was trying to teach her child the right time to say, "Yes, sir" or "Yes, ma'am". After explaining which was which, she asked, "What would you say to Mommy?" The little lad carefully replied, "Yes, ma'am." "And to Daddy?" she asked. Getting the hang of it, he replied, "Yes, sir."

Just as a final test, the mother asked, "And what would you say to Grandma?" Without a second thought, he answered, "Can I have a cookie?"

It's good to raise children with manners and respect, but it's also good for them to have somewhere they can go to be loved unconditionally.

And if there's one thing better than knowing you have a cookie waiting, it must surely be being the grandparent who provides it!

Friday — **January 16**

SALLY and Freddie arrived home after a walking holiday not so long ago. They had spent their break trekking along a long-distance footpath.

"We had some lovely weather," Sally said, "but the thing I appreciated most of all was the large number of signs and way-marks along the route. Some were very obvious, and some were quite small, but it was always reassuring to know that we were on the right track." She paused thoughtfully and then gave a sudden smile. "A bit like life, I suppose."

I like that idea. So often, when we are lost or unsure of what to do, we happen across someone who, maybe quite unwittingly, can confirm we're doing well, or perhaps point out other directions we hadn't considered.

Watch out for the way-markers of life. I'm sure you will recognise them when you come across them. And you might even be one yourself!

Saturday — January 17

IT was a wet day and I was hurrying home. But Harry was a friend, and, that day, a friend in need. He was changing his car's tyre by the roadside. I would have expected anyone to be a bit grumpy in that position, but I should have known Harry better than that.

As he flung the flat tyre in his boot he grinned at me like we were both out for a summer stroll. I commented on his cheerfulness and he agreed.

"To tell you the truth, I was doing a bit of grumbling," he admitted, "but then I realised that my bad attitude was like the car tyre – I wasn't going to get anywhere until I changed it!"

Sunday — January 18

GOD put a rainbow in the sky after the Flood as a symbol of his new covenant with mankind – a sign we may consider a reminder of his constant presence.

And if that thought isn't enough to make you smile, then think about Freya, who asked her mum if God really made the rainbow. When her mum assured her that he did, her eyes widened and she said, "Wow! God must have the biggest crayons in the world!"

Monday — January 19

THE great composer Beethoven once said, "I feel as if I have written no more than a few notes."

In one sense he was right. After all, there are only eight notes, plus variations, in the musical scale! But what made Beethoven so wonderful was the way he used those notes!

In the same way we all, from celebrities to street sweepers, have only a limited selection of responses to life's problems. Some will choose to "B Flat" but some will make beautiful music for others to enjoy. Your life is all about how you use those notes!

Tuesday — January 20

THE book was on a subject that interested me, but it was a tatty old thing. The spine was missing and the body of it hung loosely between two worn covers. But I bought it! Why? Well, on turning to the first page, someone had written the old Scottish proverb, "Do not judge by appearances; a rich heart may be under a poor coat."

Of course, the saying applies to more than just books, and I will endeavour to remember that the next time I meet someone wearing "a poor coat".

Wednesday — January 21

FROM early days, we're often told
Not to waste time at play,
That life is far too serious
To fritter it away.
But with each year that passes by
Such views begin to irk,
For I find time's too valuable
To spend it all on work.
We should leave time to stand and stare
And smell the roses' scent,
And marvel at our wondrous world.
Yes – that is time well spent!
                    Margaret Ingall.

Thursday — January 22

SOMEONE once said: "The rule of nature is living for others. The sun doesn't keep its own heat, the trees don't keep their own fruit, and flowers don't keep their fragrance to themselves. All these things are given for the benefit of others."

That seems like a rule worth keeping to me!

Friday — **January 23**

I'M sure the coach of the football team wanted them to win – but it seems he thought other things were equally important. Instead of having the boys' names printed on their shirts, he had them choose the character trait or the thing they thought was the most important.

So the boys went on to the pitch with words like "Respect", "Fairness" and "Family" on their backs. I wonder if it made a difference? If we wore our priorities on our shirts for the world to see, what would they be?

Saturday — **January 24**

THERE'S a story I would like to share with you from Lettie Cowman's classic daily devotional, "Springs In The Valley". A traveller journeying through the jungles of Africa had enlisted tribesmen to help carry his loads. On the first day they marched quickly and covered a great distance, but on the second morning the tribesmen refused to move; they simply sat and rested. When he asked about this odd behaviour, the traveller was informed that they had gone too fast the first day and were now waiting for their souls to catch up with their bodies.

In conclusion, Lettie Cowman said, "This whirling, rushing life which so many of us live does for us what that first march did for those poor jungle tribesmen. The difference: they knew what was needed to restore life's balance; too often we do not."

Sunday — **January 25**

A FRIEND who had attended a Christian youth festival noticed this slogan on a T-shirt worn by a young believer:

"Faith is not about everything turning out OK; faith is about being OK no matter how things turn out."

Monday — January 26

THE Spanish like to design decorative ceramic wall tiles with sayings or amusing notices on them. One which appealed to me was seen in a restaurant in Madrid. It said, "If you think you can sing, sing outside in the street!" Perhaps the restaurant had had some bad experiences!

However, we should not be deterred from enjoying ourselves, despite one tile's advice. So let me design my own, which would say, "Sing your own song. Dance the dance inside of you."

Go on – enjoy today with a little song and a dance! Let yourself go!

Tuesday — January 27

RECYCLE

DISCARDED rubbish has its worth,
So love the planet – save the Earth.
Bottles, cardboard, paper, tins
Taken out to wheelie bins,
Showing that the people care
When in recycling they all share.
Just love the world you're living in,
By walking to the nearest bin!
Kathleen Gillum.

Wednesday — January 28

ON a visit to a primary school I saw a motto written by an eight-year-old girl. It read, "Happiness is like jam. If you try to spead even a little you're going to get some on yourself."

If I ever meet that clever child I must tell her that I have the same problem myself!

Thursday — **January 29**

I HAPPENED to be watching a television programme recently when I was particularly struck by the words of a completely unknown elderly lady living in a tiny village in a distant country. After undergoing a charity-sponsored operation to remove long-endured cataracts, she opened her eyes and a slow smile of pure joy crept across her face. "My heart is filled with light," she marvelled.

Just six simple words, but they raise my spirits every time I think of them. May we never take for granted miracles around us, nor the people who enable us to appreciate them.

Friday — **January 30**

THE parcel was too big for the letterbox and I had been out when the postie called, so I walked to the post office the next morning. On the way, I remembered an old Russian saying: "Every day is a messenger from God."

That message is sent without fail, but it is up to us to receive it, and not leave it hanging, neglected, from the letterbox, or leave it to be picked up another day. Let's receive it like a letter from a loved one, poring over every word, and then holding it to our hearts. Get the message?

Saturday — **January 31**

SOMEONE had told Mary that the secret of happiness was low expectations. Knowing she would not have let that pass, I asked how she had responded.

"I told them, if I have low expectations and they all come true, it won't amount to much. But if I have the highest possible expectations and even a fraction come true, I will have more happiness than I can handle. And the world has never failed to live up to what I expect from it."

Neither have you, Mary, neither have you!

SIGNS OF SPRING

February

HARRY looked round as I approached. "I knew it was you from your footsteps," he said. Of course, I had to ask how my footsteps sounded. "Firm but with a slight bounce," he said with a laugh. We talked of other friends whose footsteps were "briskly purposeful" and "gently wandering" and so on.

Later I found this Native American blessing and it reminded me that even the way we walk can be a prayer.

"Let us walk softly on the earth with all living beings great and small, remembering as we go that one God, kind and wise, created all."

WE have a friend who knows how fond I am of quotations and how I enter them into my anthology. She is pleased when she discovers another one and arrived the other day with the following which was new to us both.

"It will be all right in the end, and if it's not all right, it's not the end."

I felt the unknown writer was an optimist. So often we tend to look at things and situations in our lives and think we have reached a finale.

I remember someone who used to say, "Well, that's the end of another chapter." Perhaps that was true, but it certainly wasn't the end of the book!

So the next time you feel a chapter in your life may be drawing to a conclusion, remind yourself of those words, and if it isn't all right, it is not the end! Perhaps it may be time to look for a new beginning and a fresh new start.

Tuesday — February 3

THERE'S nothing brighter or more beautiful on a rainy day than a big rainbow. They are simply stunning with their perfect arcs. The American poet and author Maya Angelou might well have been gazing at a rainbow when she penned the thought: *"Be a rainbow in someone else's cloud."*

In other words, cheer up someone who is under the weather. Do it today!

Wednesday — February 4

DREAMS

IF you would have your dreams come true
In bed you must not stay,
For dreams that never see the light
Are apt to fade away.
They need hard work and effort and
Foundations strong and deep,
And that will never happen if
You choose to oversleep.
So up and at 'em – rise and shine,
Attack those plans with zest.
It's when your dream has been fulfilled
It's time to take your rest!

Margaret Ingall.

Thursday — February 5

WHAT does memory have to do with friendship? Just that it is what keeps friendship alive and fresh even when the friends concerned may be separated by miles or years.

Sir Thomas More, Henry VIII's chancellor, must have agreed. Referring to the rosemary in his garden, he wrote, "I let it runne all over my garden wall, because 'tis a herb sacred to remembrance – and therefore to friendship."

Friday — **February 6**

GEORGE tells me his five-year-old niece found a peacock feather in the grounds of a stately home they were visiting one day and thought it beautiful.

"Didn't it hurt when it came out?" she asked.

Maybe she was thinking of a tooth she had lost recently, but George explained that the peacocks shed their feathers all the time and never noticed.

"Now isn't that a way to live?" he asked me. "Leaving beauty behind for others to enjoy; doing it so often that you are not even aware of it any more."

And the burden that would place on any life, I thought, would be light as a feather.

Saturday — **February 7**

GO placidly amidst the noise and the haste, and remember what peace there may be in silence."

They are the opening lines of that famous prose poem "Desiderata", written in 1927 by American Max Ehrmann. The words of the poem are increasingly relevant to today's world.

The poem goes on: "Be at peace with God, whatever you conceive Him to be. And whatever your labours and aspirations, in the noisy confusion of life, keep peace in your soul."

Merely reading this thought-provoking work instils a feeling of calm.

Sunday — **February 8**

SOMETIMES the start of another week can be daunting. We may have tasks to accomplish, appointments to keep and visits to make.

The only way, I find, is to take one day at a time. For many years I have used a bookmark, which now looks a little crumpled, but the words upon it are well worth remembering.

"Lord, thou knowest how busy I may be today. If I forget thee, do not thou forget me; For Christ's sake. Amen."

BEST OF FRIENDS

Monday — **February 9**

SOMETIMES music can make us want to get up and dance – although decorum may compel us to sit still and just enjoy!

Can you imagine feeling that way without music? Well, there is something else that can provide the same stimulation. The 17th-century poet George Herbert put his finger on it when he wrote, "He that lives in hope danceth without music."

May you always have enough hope in your life to make you feel like dancing – or at least like happily tapping your feet!

Tuesday — **February 10**

CAN we go it alone in this world and just depend on ourselves? If anyone could then adventurer Bear Grylls would be a good bet. He has climbed Mount Everest, explored Antarctica and lived off the land in many hostile environments.

When a young admirer asked how to be like him, Grylls replied, "Be brave when scared, endure when tired." He said there were two things every adventurer needed – good friends and strong faith.

It seems even a bear of a man needs someone to depend on!

Wednesday — **February 11**

YOU envy someone's lifestyle?
It's tempting, it is true,
To count another's blessings
And wish you had them, too.
But stop and think a moment;
It's yours you need to count,
For once you start, you'll realise
You've got the same amount!
All blessings are allotted,
We get just what we need,
Enjoy what you've been given,
And life is rich indeed.
                                    Margaret Ingall.

Thursday — February 12

IMAGINE if someone opened a bank account in your name and paid into it regularly. The only stipulation would be that you had to use the money to help your neighbours.

Then you discovered that all your neighbours had similar accounts specifically designed to help you! How wonderful would that be?

According to the theologian John Calvin, it has already happened.

"All the blessings we enjoy," he wrote, "are Divine deposits, committed to our trust on this condition, that they should be dispensed for the benefit of our neighbours."

Friday — February 13

WALKING out earlier we met Belle, the ten-year-old daughter of a friend. She told us she had started piano lessons, but didn't say how well she was doing.

That's when the Lady of the House passed on some advice from her own piano teacher. "Don't worry if you hit a wrong note. The note after that might be wonderful – but you'll never know if you let one wrong note stop you."

I filed that away, to be remembered when I hit the many wrong notes in my personal recital!

Saturday — February 14

LES and Jane are a happy couple who have been married for many years, so I was surprised to hear Jane castigating Les.

"He forgets important dates that I've told him to keep free," she said. "And he forgets that we have a long list of things to do."

"No, actually, my memory is perfect," Les replied with a smile. He gave his wife a knowing wink. "It's just that Jane and I have an all-year-round communication problem. She's always talking – and I'm never listening!"

FRAGILE BEAUTY

Sunday — **February 15**

FRAZER was telling me about a 250-mile sponsored walk he'd agreed to take part in. "It seemed like fun till I actually sat down and thought about it," he said. "Then panic set in!"

But Frazer had a friend who reminded him that even the most exciting ventures can seem overwhelming if not broken down into manageable chunks. "He suggested I take each day as it came and that's exactly what I did," Frazer said. "Sometimes it's the old advice that works best."

Indeed it does, and that's because it's true. One step at a time is a good way to tackle any challenge. And, as Frazer discovered, it will get you there in the end!

Monday — **February 16**

WHEN Charlie moved to a smaller house, he missed his garden. So he volunteered at a local hostel, taking a neglected corner of their land and turning it into a vegetable garden. Cleaned and washed, the produce is left in the kitchen for any of the residents to use.

In the shed Charlie uses for his tools (and relaxation!) is a quote from the poet Rumi. It reads: "Every leaf that grows will tell you, what you sow will bear fruit. So, if you have any sense, my friend, don't plant anything but love."

Tuesday — **February 17**

HE said, "Consider the lilies of the field."
When I remember
These simple, precious words
My minutes,
Hours,
And days
Unwind with gentleness
And quiet purpose –
Unhurried,
And all is well.
Rachel Wallace-Oberle.

Wednesday — **February 18**

THE other day the Lady of the House and I paid a visit to the ancient city of Durham. After a while, seeking time for a little reflection, we entered the Church of St Nicholas in the Market Place. Imagine the solace we felt when we saw, inscribed in a sunlit-yellow scroll, the words, "Come unto me all ye that are heavy laden and I will give you rest". With a promise such as this, who could be heavy laden for very long?

Thursday — **February 19**

SOMETIMES we feel a little daunted by a new task or challenge, perhaps even a little fearful. Christopher Columbus summed things up this way:

"You can never cross that ocean unless you have the courage to lose sight of the shore."

The majority of us will never undertake a great exploration or an epic journey. But life itself can be quite an adventure.

When the future looks to be filled with uncertainty and you are not sure what lies ahead, remember the intrepid explorer and his great courage.

Now and then we need to lose sight of the shore and sail out into the unknown. Who knows what new worlds and wonderful things we may discover!

Friday — **February 20**

MY grandmother always thinks carefully before expressing her opinion. She claims those few moments of contemplation have saved her many times from saying something she would later regret.

One of her favourite Scripture verses is Psalm 141: 3-4: "Set a guard, O Lord, over my mouth; keep watch over the door of my lips."

Words to live by each day, indeed.

Saturday — February 21

IF only we could see that we are surrounded with blessings even in the most mundane moments of our lives.

In J.M. Barrie's "A Window In Thrums", Jess's health and age mean that she spends her days in a chair, by the window of the title. Recalling her sprightly youth and a farmer she looked after, she proclaimed herself much more fortunate than him. He had been an invalid who spent days and nights in his chair, while she could get to her own bed at the end of each day.

"Mebbe ye think I'm no' much better off than Sam'l," she said, "but that's a terrible mistake. Whit a glory it wid hae been to him if he could hae gone frae one end o' the kitchen tae the ither."

I'm sure he would have thought it a wonderful thing indeed. And it makes me ask – how many unsuspected glories surround each of us any moment of any day?

Sunday — February 22

WRITER George Prochnik has always had a passion for silence. In his book, "In Pursuit Of Silence: Listening For Meaning In A Noisy World", Prochnik leaves New York City and goes on a global quest to find those who value silence. He examines the sounds that bombard us each day – air conditioners, traffic, sirens, noisy neighbours – and researches the scientific effects of noise on our bodies. Prochnik says that there is a long association with noise and hearing loss and that studies show that noise can raise our blood pressure.

While visiting a monastery, Prochnik learned that absolute silence doesn't exist, but quiet spaces are essential, because they "can inject us with a fertile unknown: a space in which to focus and absorb experience."

Take time out today to commit yourself to celebrating silence and becoming, in those moments, conscious of greater things.

"A day of silence can be a pilgrimage in itself." Hafiz.

Monday — **February 23**

WHILST travelling into town, we regularly pass a school which is very well known for its high standards. Recently we noticed a new sign had been erected near the main gates. It gave us a smile but also gave us food for thought. In large letters, the message read: "Call in and catch us doing something inspirational." What a wonderful approach!

It reminds me of a quotation I once found: "Your life is your message to the world. Make it inspiring."

Perhaps we can all try to be a little more inspiring in our own lives, and be a good example to others. I do hope so.

Tuesday — **February 24**

THE ability to tie good knots is a much under-rated talent. Ah, for the days when every child knew how to tie a bowline, a clove-hitch and a double fisherman's! But the ability to untie knots can be just as useful.

I was reminded of that by this prayer: "Dear God, please untie my knots; the will nots of my stubbornness, the can nots of my fears and the am nots of my insecurities. Then turn my heart towards the have nots of this world. And hold me to you like a reef knot, which only becomes tighter when the two ends are pulled apart."

Wednesday — **February 25**

OUT of the grey of winter
The hard of earth
A shriek of green
One single shoot
That quilts the path
Spearing the sky.

Fighting upwards
Through February sleet
Waiting to change, to break
To the love of gold
The sunlight of spring.
                    Kenneth Steven.

STILLNESS IN TIME

Thursday — **February 26**

NONE of us walks this world without sometimes feeling overwhelmed by circumstance. If, today, this is how you happen to feel, may I offer you these words from the Bible, in Romans 8:38-39: "For I am sure that neither death nor life, nor angels nor rulers, nor things present nor things to come, nor powers, nor height nor depth, nor anything else in all creation will be able to separate us from the love of God that is in Christ Jesus our Lord."

Take courage. None of us is ever truly alone or forgotten.

Friday — **February 27**

HARRY was telling me how his grandchildren had done in their school tests, and he was rightly proud of their achievements.

"I just hope as they go out into the world they pass the Angel Test." He explained it was a question his mother had asked when he was much younger. "What if the lonely people, the hurting people, the needy people are really just angels waiting to see how caring and compassionate you are?"

With Harry as a role model I'm sure his grandchildren will do just fine. And as for me, I'm off to revise for my Angel Test!

Saturday — **February 28**

IT'S often said that the old songs are the best when it comes to keeping our spirits up. One of my favourites is a little old-fashioned ditty that has inspired millions to stay happy and cheerful through difficult days. Remember this?

It's easy enough to be pleasant
When life flows by like a song,
But the man worthwhile
Is the one who will smile
When everything goes dead wrong!

Remember those lines and prove how worthwhile you are next time you hit a bad patch!

March

Sunday — **March 1**

SOMETIMES it can be easy to forget how lucky we are to be living in an age of tolerance.

When, in 1714, the Schism Act was forced through Parliament, it was specifically designed to limit religious freedom – and that was what inspired Isaac Watts to write that wonderfully reassuring hymn, "O God, Our Help In Ages Past".

O God, our help in ages past,
Our hope for years to come,
Our shelter from the stormy blast,
And our eternal home.

Simple words, yet they continue to comfort, even today.

Monday — **March 2**

A GROUP of friends were discussing the value and the importance of faith, hope and love. Our lives seem to revolve around these things and they are the support which most of us need. One person suggested that faith was the most vital ingredient to help us in all circumstances.

Another decided that hope was the most important of all – a beacon of light in our everyday living. A third person thought that love would see us through any adversity and give us the strength we need. Someone then produced this verse which appears to sum up the importance of all these things:

"Faith goes up the stairs that love has made and looks out of the window which hope has opened. "We need all of these vital ingredients to work together to make us strong; and together they make life so worthwhile.

Tuesday — **March 3**

WE started on the journey
With wonder at the world,
We skipped along with heads held high,
Our flag of hope unfurled.
Enthusiasm filled our days
As optimism grew,
We had so many plans and dreams
(Did some of them come true?)

But then our path grew steep and rough
And clouds obscured the sun,
As problems raised their worried heads
We lost our sense of fun.
But love was there through troubled times
To ease the hurt away,
With caring hands and gentle touch
It helped us through each day.

So as the road goes winding on,
Step bravely, mile by mile,
Through sun and showers, hope and joy,
The journey is worthwhile!

Iris Hesselden.

Wednesday — **March 4**

RECENTLY a large city in Scotland held its annual literary festival. The internet site to publicise the events had this quote by Lyndon Baines Johnson as its headline:

"A book is the most effective weapon against intolerance and ignorance."

Book lovers around the world will surely agree with this perceptive thought which proclaims the potential of the written word.

Thursday — **March 5**

WE did it by working together," Jeanette said, toasting the group with a cup of tea. Years before she had dreamed of having a community centre for the kids. It took a long time and a lot of hard work, but she got neighbours on board. They petitioned councillors, local businesses sponsored them, other groups joined in, and the result was a lovely new centre. Because they had worked together.

"It's like raindrops," her young daughter, Louise, put in. "By working together they make the oceans."

Louise was right. We can do a lot on our own, but we are better together.

Friday — **March 6**

WALT DISNEY was sacked by his employers at the newspaper where he worked because they said he had no imagination. The American actress Lucille Ball was dismissed from drama college for being too shy. Thomas Edison's teachers told him he was too stupid to learn anything.

These famous people might once have been viewed as hopeless in someone's eyes, but the power of failure can often result in great success.

We can learn a great life lesson from this: if you have never failed, you have never lived. Do not fear failure. No-one succeeds all the time – and who knows what successes await around the corner?

Saturday — **March 7**

THERE'S an Inuit proverb that says, "Yesterday is wood. Tomorrow is ashes. Only today does the fire burn brightly."

Let us follow their example and make each today as bright and warm as we can.

Sunday — **March 8**

PRAYER in adult life may not seem the simple thing it was in childhood. But perhaps we overcomplicate it.

Should we stand or kneel? Victor Hugo points out that "There are moments when, whatever the attitude of the body, the soul is on its knees." What do we say? Gotthold Lessing tells us, "A single grateful thought raised to heaven is the most perfect prayer."

And how do we pray in the ordinary moments of our everyday life? Samuel Taylor Coleridge suggested that "He prayeth best who loveth best."

Monday — **March 9**

THE Native Americans lived lives that were very much in touch with the earth, and now we are becoming more aware of the impact humanity has on the world perhaps we understand their wisdom a little more.

While we might delight in the beauty of the world, the Navajo tribe believed that people who appreciated the world actually added to the beauty of it. They called it "hazh'q".

Appreciating the wonder of the world around us is something for us all to aspire to. And if the Navajo are right, there would be a bonus for our efforts. For in appreciating wonder and beauty, it seems we make the world a more wonderful and more beautiful place!

Tuesday — **March 10**

RECORD producer and composer Quincy Jones knows a thing or two about harmony. It was he who said, "Imagine what a harmonious world it could be if every single person, both young and old, shared a little of what they are good at doing."

So why not find out what you're good at – and there will be lots of things – and join in the music!

Wednesday — **March 11**

ARE you facing a particular challenge today? I suspect most of us will be, whether it's a major mental or physical hurdle or something so minor we can almost take it in our stride. So here are a few encouraging thoughts.

"It always seems impossible until it's done." Nelson Mandela.

"If you lack the courage to start, you have already finished." Anon.

"I have always grown from my problems and challenges; from the things that don't work out, that's when I've really learned." Carol Burnett.

Good luck!

Thursday — **March 12**

TEACH me to pray, Father,
Teach me humbly to kneel,
To be still,
To stop asking,
To listen.
Teach me to wait,
Quietly,
Gratefully.
Teach me to give thanks,
And stand upon your faithful answers of yesterday
Rather than falter before tomorrow's needs.
Teach me to say, "Amen",
With confidence,
Trusting you have heard
And cannot fail me.
Teach me to pray, Father,
Not with words,
But with my heart.
Rachel Wallace-Oberle.

Friday — **March 13**

THE Italians have a proverb which says, "At the end of the game, the king and the pawn go back in the same box."

People might see themselves as being more important than others, but we should not overrate ourselves as, at the end of the day, we all end up in the same place anyway!

Saturday — **March 14**

AS an illustrator of children's books, my great-aunt Louisa was very interested in all forms of art. An entry in her diary for March 14 read, "*Ars Longa, Vita Brevis*. I discovered today that this means art is long, life is short. Does this mean that after I die, my art will live on for many years? I do hope so! But I would prefer if life were perhaps not so short – I have so much art to give, so I had better not waste a single minute!"

Sunday — **March 15**

TODAY mothers are celebrating a very special occasion set aside for them.

Although Mother's Day has different origins in other parts of the world, most have been influenced by an American tradition established by Ann Jarvis in 1868. She created a committee to establish a "Mothers' Friendship Day" in order to reunite families that had been divided during the Civil War.

Though Ann passed away before the celebration became popular, her daughter continued her mother's efforts and eventually a day was set aside to recognise the special contributions of mothers.

Kate Douglas Wiggin, American educator and children's author, said, "Most all the beautiful things in life come by twos and threes, by dozens and hundreds. Plenty of roses, stars, sunsets, rainbows, brothers and sisters, aunts and cousins – but only one mother in the whole wide world."

BURSTING FORTH

Monday — **March 16**

A FRIEND recently bought the old straight-backed minister's chair that had been lying in his church's storeroom for years. Sure as I am that the church will put his donation to good use, I had to question his wisdom.

The chair was scuffed and scored, I knew it wouldn't match the rest of the furniture in his house, and I dared to suggest that it didn't even look very comfortable!

"You're probably right," he conceded. "But imagine all the thoughts of God that have been thought in it!"

It was my turn to concede. There are many different ways to be comfortable; I suppose resting in thoughts of God has to be one of the best!

Tuesday — **March 17**

LETTER TO A FRIEND

I HAVEN'T written for a while,
(The weeks all slip away),
And yet I still remember you
And think of you each day.
I think of all the times we've shared,
They live on in my heart,
The memories all bring you close,
We're never far apart.

I hope that you are safe and well,
And life is good and kind.
I pray the troubles of the past
Are simply left behind.
And so accept this letter now
With all the love I send,
And though the years go swiftly by,
I'll always be your friend.

Iris Hesselden.

Wednesday — **March 18**

ERIC GILL, who lived in the first half of the 20th century, was an artist with a special talent. He was a "letterist", decorating text and engraving words in wood. He took the lesson from his particular ability when he wrote, "Every artist may not be a special kind of person, but every person is a special kind of artist."

We can all add to the beauty of the world in a unique way – once we find what we do best.

Thursday — **March 19**

WORDSWORTH'S poem, "Daffodils", is one of the most famous pieces of poetry ever. But he was not alone on the trip that inspired, "When all at once I saw a crowd, a host of golden daffodils."

His sister, Dorothy, wrote in her diary, "I never saw daffodils so beautiful. They grew among the mossy stones about them. Some rested their heads on the stones, as on a pillow, for weariness; the rest tossed and danced, and seemed as if they verily laughed with the wind that blew over the lake.

Isn't it reassuring to know that you don't have to be a great poet in order to appreciate great beauty?

Friday — **March 20**

MORNING, Francis!" Ben said as I passed his house. "What do you think of my new front wall, then?" It was certainly a handsome piece of work, and I had to admire the speed with which it had been done.

"I did have some help," he admitted. "Two friends came to stay, who are not only wonderful at DIY, but were equally keen to help me with the job. In fact, they were such good tutors that I was able to finish it all by myself!"

Well, that does sound like a friendship built on firm foundations!

Saturday — **March 21**

HOW many of us like problems? I don't imagine many hands went up when I asked that question. But perhaps the problem with problems lies more in our approach to them than anything else.

Buckminster Fuller, the inventor, said, "When I'm working on a problem, I never think about beauty. I think only how to solve the problem. But when I have finished, if the solution is not beautiful, I know it is wrong."

We might like problems more if we saw them as Mr Fuller did, as opportunities to bring more beauty to the world!

Sunday — **March 22**

SALLY was chatting to the Lady of the House about a new hairdressing salon she had visited. "The haircut was fine," she said, "but, oh, sitting reading magazines about celebrities did make me feel inadequate!"

We laughed, for we knew Sally wasn't really serious. And yet, sadly, if we are feeling at all vulnerable, it can be much too easy to compare our lives to others' and feel ourselves failures. If this happens to apply to you, remember these words from Job 33:4: "The Spirit of God hath made me, and the breath of the Almighty hath given me life."

I think that qualification makes every one of us a superstar!

Monday — **March 23**

TALKING about "high thoughts" versus "low thoughts", the author G.K. Chesterton suggested the very highest form of thought ought to be the giving of thanks, or gratitude. It was, he declared, "happiness doubled by wonder."

Those are the kind of delightful "high thoughts" that anyone could think. Indeed, who could ever wish to think any other kind?

BORGUND
STAVE CHURCH,
NORWAY

Tuesday — **March 24**

I'VE been reading about Pierre Teilhard de Chardin, the French priest and philosopher whose interests ranged from palaeontology to cosmology.

He was born in 1881 and led a life full of travel, action and achievement, notably winning the Legion of Honour for valour. He also published many books on mankind's place in the universe, some of which were regarded as a little too radical at the time.

But he is certainly a fascinating subject and some words of his which I particularly like are these.

"We are not human beings having a spiritual experience. We are spiritual beings having a human experience."

Now that's a way of looking at things that's definitely worth thinking about.

Wednesday — **March 25**

HAVE you ever heard the phrase, "You can never be home again"? I suppose it is about growing up, losing innocence and so on.

But it takes no account of the fact that this world was made for you and you were made to live in it wherever you might be.

Maya Angelou hit the nail on the head when she said, "You can never go home again, but the truth is you can never leave home, so it's all right!"

Thursday — **March 26**

HERE are a few quotes about art which inspired Great-aunt Louisa, a keen artist:

"A picture is a poem without words." *Horace*

"A good painting to me has always been like a friend. It keeps me company, comforts and inspires." *Hedy Lamarr*

"All art is but imitation of nature." *Seneca*

Friday — **March 27**

I HAD to laugh at the delightful video clip one of my friends showed me on the internet. Two little flower girls were walking down the aisle at a wedding. Both carried pretty baskets. One, a girl of probably about eight or nine, was scattering rose petals from her basket.

The other little flower girl, though, was only about three, and she was running after the older one picking up all the petals and putting them in her own basket! The assembled family and friends thought it was adorable. And it was – but it made me think.

A bride should have her petals as she walks down the aisle. But for the rest of us, let's not cast away the little wonders of our days away without even looking back, when really we should be gathering them up and cherishing them.

Saturday — **March 28**

IN the stillness of a garden
The spirit is refreshed,
The soul responds to beauty
And is richly blessed.
It's where the heart finds healing
When weary and subdued
Through the peace and quietness
And calming solitude.
A garden is a sanctuary,
A place where we may be
Alone with God to ponder on
Nature's mystery.
To see in green and growing things,
In flower, bird and tree,
The Mind behind the universe
In creativity.
                        Kathleen Gillum.

DAFT ABOUT DAFFS

Sunday — **March 29**

A PSYCHIATRIST was asked to sum up what his work was all about. "It becomes more and more clear to me," he said, "that most of my patients are really just people trying different ways to get someone to love them."

"Isn't everyone like that?" he was asked.

"I don't think so," he replied. "There are people I never see. I guess they are the ones out there doing the loving."

And it becomes more and more clear to me that the best thing we can ever do, for ourselves and for others, is to love!

"Finally, all of you, be like-minded, be sympathetic, love one another, be compassionate and humble." 1 Peter 3:8.

Monday — **March 30**

"YOU KNOW," Harry said, "they talk about pessimists seeing the glass as half empty and optimists seeing the glass as half full. But it's the optimists who have it right."

I waited for Harry to explain the age-old dilemma.

"The bottom half is full of water," he said, "but the top half is full of air. You wouldn't say a car tyre was empty, would you? So the glass is always full! The blessings of life are like that. Some you see and some you don't, but life is always full of them!"

I walked away thinking that sometimes Harry just makes my glass run over!

Tuesday — **March 31**

DON QUIXOTE said to his squire, Sancho Panza, "There is no such thing as an untrue proverb." Here is a Spanish one with more than a grain of truth.

"He who sows courtesy reaps friendship, and he who plants kindness gathers love."

April

DOROTHY received a card through the post from her friend, Anna, who lives many miles away. Anna knew her friend was going through a bad time, and on the card these words were written:
"Time passes.
Life happens.
Distance separates.
Children grow up.
Jobs come and go.
Love waxes and wanes.
Hearts break. Careers end.

"But friends are there, no matter how much time has passed or how many miles are between you. A friend is never farther away than needing her can reach. When you have to walk that lonely valley, your friend will be on the valley's edge, cheering you on, praying for you, waiting with open arms. Some will even break the rules and walk beside you, or come in and carry you out."

Truly, the world would not be the same without friends!

Thursday — **April 2**

IT'S often said that if we have friends we are rich. Of course, friends don't add to our bank balance, but they add to the ordinary moments of life, enriching them in the most delightful ways.

The ancient Chinese had a saying that summed up the value friendships add to life.

"With true friends even water, if drunk together, is sweet enough!"

Friday — **April 3**

A SINGLE act of kindness throws out roots in all directions, and the roots spring up and make new trees. The greatest work that kindness does to others is that it makes them kind themselves."

If you are reading those words and assuming they come from some famous philosopher, think again. They are some thoughts of that courageous pioneer of early flight, Amelia Earhart. Which proves, I think, that she may have had her head in the air, but her feet were most firmly on the ground!

Saturday — **April 4**

I WONDERED what the poet Robert Bridges meant when he wrote "Friendship is in loving rather than being loved." Shouldn't we want to have friends as well as be one?

Then it dawned on me. It's one of life's paradoxes that the more we focus on being a good friend, the more people will want to be good friends to us!

Sunday — **April 5**

A LLELUIA! Easter morning,
Hear the bells ring out,
Feel the joy and new upliftment
Banish fear and doubt.
Alleluia! Gone the darkness,
Feel the hope within,
Onward to a bright tomorrow
See the way begin.
Alleluia! Share the gladness,
Joy be unconfined,
Gifts of wonder, love and beauty
Filling heart and mind.
Alleluia! He is risen
Farewell darkest night,
Death and sadness gone for ever,
Welcome Love and Light!
                              Iris Hesselden.

Monday — **April 6**

WHAT would you do if God tapped you on the shoulder? It's a difficult concept to imagine, I know, but hopefully you will have experienced something the playwright Charles Morgan considered to be very closely related.

"There is no surprise," he wrote, "like the surprise of being loved. It is the finger of God on one's shoulder."

Tuesday — **April 7**

ONE of Albert Einstein's pupils commented that the great man had never been particularly good at maths. What made the difference was his ability to immerse himself in a problem until he solved it.

The best friends to have when you are struggling aren't necessarily those with the most money or useful contacts. The best friends are the ones who, like Einstein, will immerse themselves in your problem till they have helped solve it.

Wednesday — **April 8**

AT a time when we are all being urged to recycle as much as possible, I wonder if you, like me, happened to catch a TV programme in which a small team of musical instrument makers were challenged to transform a selection of junk into an orchestra.

The task was daunting. The craftsmen were uncertain that they'd be able to make instruments of high enough quality. The musicians feared they would end up looking foolish.

Much perseverance and trust was needed. But the result? A rendition of the "1812 Overture" that prompted a standing ovation at the Royal Albert Hall. Which just goes to show, I think, that even from a scrapheap beautiful music can still emerge!

Thursday — **April 9**

"THERE are eight steps to overcoming a problem," a friend once told me. "They are, 'I won't do it', 'I can't do it', 'I want to do it', 'How do I do it?', 'I'll try to do it', 'I can do it', 'I will do it' and 'Hooray, I did it'!

"Improvement is only ever one step away, and soon you'll have the problem solved. Just concentrate on what you'd like to achieve and, before you know it, you'll have succeeded."

Friday — **April 10**

"AND what do you do?" Have you noticed that whenever we are asked that question we invariably reply in terms of our work? The great violinist, Yehudi Menuhin, wondered why it was that we let our paid employment define us.

"Why shouldn't a person just be enjoying life, and contributing in his own way by going and visiting people he likes, or doing some work without pay, or being an amateur at something?"

Work is important, but there are other things that matter more. With that in mind, may I ask again: "What do you do?"

Saturday — **April 11**

DESPITE being born in Germany, Carl Schurz fought in the American Civil War and went on to become one of that country's most famous politicians. He was known for never toeing a party line and, instead, always following his conscience.

Once, he was asked about the value of ideals in a materialistic world. His answer was worth hearing then, and is still worth hearing today.

"Ideals are like stars," he said. "You will not succeed in touching them, but like seafaring men, you choose them as your guides and, following them, you will reach your destiny."

Sunday — **April 12**

FOLK often use the term "spitting image" to talk about how similar things or people are. Actually, the correct term is "spirit and image", which, when you stop to think about it, makes much more sense.

It may not be physically possible for many of us to resemble Jesus, but we can show him to the world in our words and deeds. And what's the best way to do that? To be as like him as we possibly can be – in spirit if not in image.

Monday — **April 13**

AS well as being a great writer and satirist, Thomas Carlyle was also a great teacher. A student once wrote to ask how he, too, might become such a teacher. Carlyle replied, "Be what you would have your students be."

It reminded me of St Francis of Assisi's advice to his students. He said, "It is no use walking anywhere to preach unless walking *is* preaching."

If we would prefer those around us to be better, nicer and more helpful, then we might teach them how: not by telling them, but by showing them!

Tuesday — **April 14**

LET us try to cultivate
The art of being still,
For it's when the nerves are frayed
That we start feeling ill.
In the tranquil, healing calm
The spirit is renewed,
The petty irritations
Are quietened and subdued.
A gentle peace steals on the soul
And we are richly blessed,
Once more our jaded spirits
Are uplifted and refreshed.
                    Kathleen Gillum.

Wednesday — **April 15**

A LITTLE boy was learning the piano and, to encourage him, his mother took him to hear a famous musician give a recital. While his mother chatted to a friend before the concert began, the boy slipped out of his seat and decided to explore. No sooner had the mother returned to her seat and realised her son had gone than the curtains opened and, to her horror, she saw him sitting at the piano on stage picking out "Twinkle, Twinkle, Little Star".

Quietly, the piano master came on stage and whispered, "Don't stop." Leaning over, with his left hand he began filling in a bass line, then his right hand played a running obligato. Together the master and novice transformed an awkward situation into a wonderful creative experience, mesmerising the audience.

At times, what we can accomplish on our own seems little, but with a helping hand we can all achieve great things.

Thursday — **April 16**

D URING his lifetime, J.S. Bach was a renowned organist, but his compositions went largely ignored.

Then, 80 years after his death, Felix Mendelssohn found music amongst a box of papers that choristers had been wrapping their lunches in. The music was found to be Bach's Easter composition, "St Matthew Passion". Mendelssohn made sure Bach's "Hidden Music" was performed in Berlin – the restoration of Bach's reputation as a composer had begun.

The fact that no-one was interested in hearing his music didn't stop Bach composing. In the same way, just because we can't always see the effect it has, this shouldn't stop us putting a little love and kindness into a troubled world. It might not seem worthwhile at the time but, like Bach's "Hidden Music", it might just be waiting for the right time to be heard.

RADIANT RHODODENDRONS

Friday — **April 17**

MOST of the American states have a slogan they advertise themselves with. Georgia is the "Peach State", for example, and Delaware calls itself the "Small Wonder."

But Utah (which has mountains and a skiing industry) describes itself as "Life Elevated". We should all try to lead such a life – whether in Utah or not!

Saturday — **April 18**

I HAVE just added a new word to my vocabulary – a rather unusual one, which came to me in an e-mail from a friend.

The word is "paraprosdokian", which means a figure of speech in which the latter part of a sentence surprises or is unexpected; often used humorously.

My paraprosdokian for today is: "Going to church doesn't make you a Christian any more than standing in a garage makes you a car!"

Worth a thought, I'd say!

Sunday — **April 19**

ON one of my walks there's a spot where a little electrical substation used to be. All around is long grass, but the broken bricks and rubble left behind seem to have caught wildflower seeds and now it's a garden in the grass.

Each time I see it I think of the Persian poet, Rumi, who said, "Be crumbled. So wild flowers will come up where you are. You have been too stony for too many years. Try something different."

Being strong, determined and serious has its place in life. But try something different once in a while, and see what might grow.

Monday — **April 20**

"IF something's not perfect, then throw it away!"
That's always the message I'm hearing today.
"Don't spend any effort on putting it right –
Just go get a new one that's shiny and bright."
But, oh, I say no to such notions bizarre,
I like all my things just the way that they are:
The shabby old armchair, the battered old books,
So what if they're scruffy? Who cares for their looks?
And even the friends whom I love to call by –
They're not new or perfect, and neither am I.
So scoff if you will, for there's one thing I'll say:
I've things in my life I just won't throw away!

Margaret Ingall.

Tuesday — **April 21**

THE village green was unusually busy with people when I passed, so when Ted waved me over I was happy to pause and satisfy my curiosity.

"We're doing a litter-pick, Francis," he told me. "The green has been looking scruffy lately, so we all agreed to come and do our part to make it good again."

The sight of so many willing volunteers cheered me, and certainly brought to mind those words of Albert Schweitzer: "You must give some time to your fellow men. Even if it's a little thing, do something for others – something for which you get no pay but the privilege of doing it."

Wednesday — **April 22**

ARTHUR CONAN DOYLE, author of the Sherlock Holmes novels, wrote, "I consider that a man's brain originally is like a little empty attic, and you have to stock it with such furniture as you choose." We can fill our "little attics" with good furniture or bad, but the good will always last longer.

Thursday — **April 23**

THE boat was long and sleek and looked beautiful in the sunshine. It was being towed by a car which was not quite as sleek or immaculate.

The family appeared to be heading towards the coast, and I thought how wonderful it must be to go sailing in such a delightful craft.

The driver of the car stopped for petrol and we were able to take a closer look. Always curious about the names people choose for boats, I particularly wanted to see this one. Imagine my surprise when I saw the lettering, very carefully done: *Reallycouldn'tdecide.*

I thought how many times in our lives we have to make decisions, and how difficult they can often be. Perhaps, instead of rushing ahead and making the wrong choice, we should take time – pause and consider the problem.

Like the owner of the boat, we can continue with our lives while giving ourselves a little more time to decide.

Friday — **April 24**

HARRY and I were talking with a man who informed us he was a collector.

"I have albums full of foreign stamps, cards that used to come in tea packets, even albums of letters from the eighteenth century. What about you?" He directed the question at Harry. "Do you collect?"

"No," Harry told him firmly. "I recollect." He tapped his temple. "I have albums in here where I recollect beaches, churches, rivers, barns in the countryside, friends and kind words."

Collecting as a hobby might not be for everyone, but in recollecting Harry might just have come up with a pastime we can all enjoy!

Saturday — **April 25**

HOW easy it is to find excuses not to do something! But if, with a little belief in ourselves, we focus on finding reasons to do things, we will be amazed by how much we actually achieve!

That wonderful truth was summed up by Pierre Teilhard de Chardin, who wrote, "Our duty, as men and women, is to proceed as if limits to our ability did not exist. We are collaborators in creation."

Sunday — **April 26**

WHEN, nearly 200 years ago, vicar Reginald Heber decided to compile a list of hymns to complement the church calendar, he was stuck for one to use for Trinity Sunday, the day which reaffirms that there is one God who is Father, Son and Holy Spirit.

That's how he came to write "Holy, Holy, Holy", one of our nation's best-loved hymns.

And it's far too good to save for just one day a year.

Monday — **April 27**

STROLLING through Glasgow's beautiful botanic gardens, I couldn't help noticing the Cyathea robertsiana – specifically the plaque which told me the plant grows best in disturbed ground – where there had been landslips, for instance.

It grows quickly, its leaves shelter the soil and its roots help hold the ground together.

Just like people, some plants need a firm, secure grounding, but others flourish and flower in tricky situations, working quickly to stabilise things again.

It occurred to me that I have a few friends who might easily be classed as robertsianas. And I hope you do, too!

Tuesday — **April 28**

*K*INDNESS is a gift
You're meant to give away,
So offer it to all
You pass along the way.
Its worth can never dull,
Its charm can never cloy,
It costs you not a thing,
And brings you naught but joy.
For kindness is a gift,
The sweetest and the best,
The more that you bestow,
The more your path is blessed.
                    Margaret Ingall.

Wednesday — **April 29**

IMAGINE we could be lucky enough to travel into deep space and look down on tiny Planet Earth. How would we feel about what life means?

Joseph Campbell, an American mythologist, writer and lecturer, captured it well with this quote. "The goal of life is to make your heartbeat match the beat of the universe, to match your nature with Nature."

Thursday — **April 30**

THE priest-poet George Herbert deserves to be remembered for his good deeds. Once, on his way to listen to music at a friend's house, he happened upon a poor man whose horse had fallen, spilling its load on to the dirty, muddy road. He spent so long helping the man that he arrived late for his engagement, and his clothes were now dirty and unkempt.

His friends were shocked and expressed their disgust, but Herbert only smiled and said, "The thought of what I did will be music to me at midnight." He told them he did not want to pass one day of his life without comforting a sad soul or showing mercy.

Little wonder he was so well loved.

May

A PRAYER FOR YOUR JOURNEY

MAY God go with you on your way
To keep you safe and well,
And may you find new strength and hope,
And every doubt dispel.

May God be always close to you
Whatever you may find,
And give you courage, faith and joy
And healing peace of mind.

May every path that you must take
Be smoother than before,
And lead you on to sunlit times
Till you come home once more.
Iris Hesselden.

JOHN lives in a tiny cottage in a remote part of the countryside. He works on the land, never strays far from home, and describes himself as "a dull sort of fellow".

Whoever goes to visit John is assured a warm welcome, a listening ear and, if required, a store of wise advice from an honest heart. In fact, he puts me in mind of those words by James Allen, who reminded us that "The strong, calm man is loved and revered. He is like a shade-giving tree in a thirsty land, or a sheltering rock in a storm."

Dull? I don't think so!

Sunday — **May 3**

FEEL so stupid!" Sally said. "Fancy arranging a birthday tea for Jim – on the wrong day!" Fortunately, Sally's mistake had no consequences other than some embarrassment on her part. But none of us like that horrible feeling of realising we've got something wrong, especially when it's important.

That's the time to remember the words of Isaiah, 41:10: "Fear not, for I am with you; be not dismayed, for I am your God; I will strengthen you, I will help you, I will uphold you with my righteous right hand."

We all do foolish things, but with God's help we can concentrate on getting it right next time.

Monday — **May 4**

PIERS SELLERS was an ecologist and an astronaut. He said: "The world is a big blue ball just bowling its way around space. The atmosphere is incredibly thin, like an onion skin around the Earth. It makes you think the world is very small – and there are all these people on it."

Sometimes it helps to see things from a different viewpoint. In the great scheme of things we are small and fragile, but nonetheless valuable to those who love us.

Tuesday — **May 5**

I'M sure American author Christian D. Larson inspired many when he said, "Promise yourself to be so strong that nothing can disturb your peace of mind. Look at the sunny side of everything and make your optimism come true. Think only of the best, work only for the best, and expect only the best. Forget the mistakes of the past and press on to the greater achievements of the future. Give so much time to the improvement of yourself that you have no time to criticise others. Live in the faith that the whole world is on your side as long as you are true to the best that is in you."

CALM WATERS

Wednesday — **May 6**

ROBERT LOUIS STEVENSON, the famous Scottish novelist and poet, once said, "Don't judge each day by the harvest you reap but by the seeds that you plant."

You will later have the pleasure of seeing what your seeds will grow into. So sow the seeds of friendship today without seeking anything in return, and enjoy an unexpected harvest!

Thursday — **May 7**

I CAN'T think of a more satisfactory way to spend time," Harry said, leaning on his spade, "than working in a garden."

As I admired his vegetable plot, I had to admit that the sight, and his enthusiasm, was uplifting. Of course, not everyone is lucky enough to have access either to a garden or an allotment, which was why I was interested when Harry went on to tell me about the Landshare Project.

It's a scheme which enables would-be gardeners to be put in touch with those who have unused land that they're willing to share, while tools, experience, support and produce are shared with equal generosity.

It's a wonderfully simple concept, but what an excellent one. I do hope it continues to grow!

Friday — **May 8**

BEFORE he died at the age of fifty-six, Steve Jobs, who co-founded the successful Apple company, said, "Being the richest man in the cemetery doesn't matter to me. Going to bed at night knowing we've done something wonderful, that's what matters to me."

We can't all establish a world-famous firm, but we can strive to do something meaningful each day. And, having done this, we can sleep easily in our beds knowing we have achieved something worthwhile.

Saturday — **May 9**

THERE have been times, I'm sure, when you have had your soul filled by a sunset, when a story of tenderness has brought happy tears to your eyes, when you have watched children at play and been sure this must be what heaven is like.

But what happens to that wonderful feeling afterwards? All too often it dissipates. But how would it be if we took the feelings these moments inspired and turned them into some good deed which left someone else feeling just as happy?

The Persian poet Rumi summed it up: "Let the beauty we love become the good that we do." And that wonderful feeling will be passed on, and will have a new beginning.

Sunday — **May 10**

WHAT if you walked by a river
    That sang and danced
And never remembered
Yesterday's debris?
What if you stood
Beneath a canopy of trees
That never stopped
Reaching towards heaven?
What if you knelt
Before a rose
That never doubted its purpose
To perfume each day?
What if you looked up at stars
That never faltered
At the approach of night,
Or hesitated
To outshine the dark?
Tell me, friend,
What then?

Rachel Wallace-Oberle.

Monday — **May 11**

WHILE watching the Olympics which took place in London in 2012, I heard many winning athletes admit that it had taken years of sacrifice and dedication to reach their goal.

The slogan for the 2012 Olympics was "Better never stops", meaning that improvement continues when you make the decision to work at being better at whatever it is that you do.

To be the best we can be in daily life also takes time and effort, but it is worth it for the good that comes of it, for ourselves and for others.

Tuesday — **May 12**

IN the troubled years of Oliver Cromwell's Commonwealth they do say that only one church was built in England. Above its arched entrance was inscribed *When all things sacred were, throughout the nation, either demolished or profaned, Sir Robert Shirley founded this church, whose singular praise is to have done the best things in the worst times.*

The trials we face might not be of such national significance but we make our own personal world a better place each time we follow Sir Robert's example and do the best things in the worst times.

Wednesday — **May 13**

SOMEONE (I can't help thinking he must have been a hard-nosed businessman) once said, "There is nothing, short of being shot at and missed, quite as satisfying as a tax refund."

Well – there is waking up each morning, realising you have been granted another day; saying thank you at the end of a day in which you have been of some use; a baby's hand holding tight to your finger; the look of love from your sweetheart that needs no words . . . I could go on and on.

That's not to say a tax refund wouldn't be appreciated – but the free pleasures in life are so much more satisfying!

EDZELL
CASTLE

Thursday — **May 14**

OUR friend, Mary, made me laugh the other day when she was telling us about something she had read in an article.

"It mentioned a quote from Albert Camus," she said. "'Alas, after a certain age, every man is responsible for his own face'. I must say I found that rather depressing!"

But, of course, Mary is not a person to look on the black side for long.

"Then again," she went on, "I may not have spent enough time smiling to get the face I want yet. But he didn't say what the 'certain age' was. There might still be time!"

Friday — **May 15**

YOU might expect a series of lectures on "The Chemical History Of A Candle" to be fairly dull – until you read the closing comments: "All I can say to you at the end of these lectures is to express a wish that you may, in your generation, be fit to compare to a candle; that you may, like it, shine as lights to those about you; that in all your actions you may justify the beauty of the taper by making your deeds honourable and effectual in the discharge of your duty to your fellow man."

Dull? It seems that from the great scientist Michael Faraday we should have expected what he expected of his students – something brighter!

Saturday — **May 16**

IN past times, folk never moved far away from the town they were born in. These days, travel is so much easier, and holidays to all the farthest corners of the world are commonplace.

But the most important journey any of us will take is the one that allows us to meet someone else halfway.

Sunday — **May 17**

I'M sure many people will be familiar with the song "Let there be peace on earth, and let it begin with me."

I like it not just for its lovely melody and excellent sentiment, but for that last phrase, "Let it begin with me".

It's too often that we express a wish for the world to be a better place, without it ever seeming to occur that we ourselves might be the ones to make the first move.

We don't have to be world leaders, or any kind of leaders – just willing to take that one small step that will make us feel we are doing our bit.

And who knows what might happen after that? For even the biggest snowball begins with a single snowflake.

Monday — **May 18**

MY nine-year-old nephew, Logan, had decided that he wanted to join the athletics club at school, and to enter for some of the events in an upcoming competition.

Each morning he got up early to train before school. His mother encouraged him, even though running isn't Logan's strongest suit, so his progress was slow. On the day of the event, Logan ran as fast as he could and really put everything into his race, but unfortunately he still came in last.

One of the older boys, who had been watching from the sidelines, made a point of congratulating Logan on his enthusiasm and effort. He, too, was part of the school athletics club and he understood how far my nephew had come and the progress he had made.

As a result, those words of praise and a sense of achievement were what Logan took away that day – not the disappointment of losing.

As Jonathan Lockwood Huie said, "Sometimes you get the results you wanted, sometimes you don't. What matters is you did your best."

Tuesday — **May 19**

WILLIAM PENN, who was born in London and founded the state of Pennsylvania, was known for his sense of decency and fair play.

When it came to good deeds, he wrote, "He that does good for good's sake seeks neither paradise nor reward, but he is sure of both in the end."

Wednesday — **May 20**

WRITERS often dedicate their books to someone they love or someone who has been a great help to them.

The 17th-century poet Robert Herrick did both when he wrote this dedication: "If any thing delight me for to print my book, 'tis this; that thou, my God, art in't."

Be it a book, a life, or simply what you do this day, you could do worse than dedicate it to God.

Thursday — **May 21**

AND they lived happily every after." It's the classic end to a fairy story, isn't it? And, if we're honest, it's what we all hope for in life.

Yet we only have to look around to see that none of us is lucky enough to live in a state of permanent happiness.

That is why I was so touched by the words of American actress Helen Hayes:

"The story of love is not important – what is important is that one is capable of love. It is perhaps the only glimpse we are permitted of eternity."

Oh, if only life could turn out perfectly for all of us! But if you are lucky enough to have experienced that little glimpse of eternity, hold it in your heart. It is more precious than any fairy tale could ever be.

A LITTLE COLOUR MAKES A BIG DIFFERENCE!

Friday — **May 22**

TALKING about the soul, the great Russian painter Kandinsky said, "There is nothing on earth so curious for beauty, or so absorbent of it."

If the soul absorbs beauty then let's give it every opportunity to paint itself as a masterpiece!

Saturday — **May 23**

THEY come in all shapes and all sizes,
And all sorts of colours, as well,
Some stick around for a lifetime
While others just stay for a spell.
They warm up and lighten and brighten
The pathways we walk throughout life,
Betimes they're more loyal and steadfast
Than husband or children or wife!
And always there's solace and healing
Whatever Dame Fortune may send,
In the present which heaven has sent us
All packaged up as a friend.
                    Tricia Sturgeon.

Sunday — **May 24**

THE frontiersman Davy Crockett knew the American woods and mountains like very few others did. But a biographer recalled that some of the sights he encountered still had the power to take his breath away.

"O God, what a world of beauty thou hast made for man!" Crockett once exclaimed. "And yet how poorly does he requite thee for it! He does not even repay thee with gratitude."

This world was indeed made for us. Like Crockett, we should take the time to stop and look around – and show our appreciation as often as we can.

Monday — **May 25**

JANE was telling me the other day about a new clock she had bought, and she asked me if I'd like to see it. I said I would, of course, although I couldn't quite understand why she was so keen to show it off.

The clock was certainly attractive. It was made of polished pewter, designed in an antique style, and hung on the kitchen wall on a little curlicued bracket. I gave it a brief glance and smiled at Jane.

I started to say, "Very pretty," but something caught my eye and I took a second look.

You see, when the ornate hands of this clock move around the face, they don't point to numbers or Roman numerals like most of the timepieces I am used to seeing. On this clock, where the numbers should be is the word "Now".

So, it may be five past, quarter to, or on the hour, but the time for Jane, according to her new clock, will always be the best time to get things done.

Now.

Tuesday — **May 26**

THERE are gifts you can give which are costly and rare,
Gifts you can give which take effort and care,
Gifts fun and fancy, done up with a bow,
Yet harder is one sort of gift to bestow.
For if you've been hurt or upset by a friend
The links of affection are tricky to mend.
Yet, still, if that friendship you long to recall,
Forgiveness, you'll find, is the best gift of all.
For not only will your friend be glad and rejoice,
You, too, will walk tall, for you made a good choice.

Margaret Ingall.

Wednesday — **May 27**

THERE are, in effect, two things – to know and to believe one knows. To know is science; to believe one knows is ignorance." So wrote Hippocrates, the Greek physician.

A more up-to-date version says, "A little learning is a dangerous thing."

Far safer to have a lot of learning before you voice an opinion or do something important. Ancient wisdom has a long life!

Thursday — **May 28**

THERE'S a legend of St Columba that tells how, just before the saint died, the monastery's carthorse came into his room, rested its head on him and wept. Perhaps Columba appreciated the horse more than the other monks, and was kinder to it?

Let's look out for people bearing burdens and help them – not so that they will weep for us when we are gone, but so their loads will be lighter while they live.

Friday — **May 29**

TOM grows flowers for the supermarkets and we were standing by one of his fields. Rows of beautiful blooms stretched as far as the eye could see.

"It's hard to imagine that a few months ago this was an empty field," I said. "Until you did the planting."

"Oh, there's nothing special about that," he replied. "Well, nothing special inasmuch as it's something anyone can do. People plant things in the fields of their lives every day. I just get to plant pretty things."

Tom makes his living by planting pretty things. In planting seeds of kindness, patience and love in our "fields" we get to make pretty lives, for ourselves and for others.

Saturday — **May 30**

REPEAT a piece of music often enough and people just stop hearing it. But introduce a new instrument and the piece takes on new life. The French poet Stephane Mallarme wrote, "Every soul is a melody which needs renewing."

New friends are the instruments that renew the music of our lives.

Sunday — **May 31**

OUR minister had been speaking on the text "pressed on every side by troubles, but not crushed and broken", and we came home still thinking about it. It was as if we needed some help – a picture, perhaps – to grasp the meaning properly.

We looked out of the kitchen window at the bright clump of daffodils that had burst up through the cold soil. Their yellow trumpets were turned towards us, as if sounding out some wonderful melody that only the other flowers could hear.

Then, that night, five inches of snow fell while we slept – heavy, wet snow that demolished everything in the spring garden and even clung around the white plum blossoms. What a disappointment when we looked out. There was not a daffodil in sight – all had been crushed beneath this onslaught.

But the snow did not stay long, and the daffodils reappeared: a bit squashed at first, but the blazing yellow trumpets were still there. Day by day they stood up straighter, until no-one would have known that there had been any snow at all.

"That's it!" the Lady of the House exclaimed. "From now on, we must face our troubles like a daffodil, and rise up again when we are crushed by life."

June

Monday — **June 1**

HAVE you ever been to a village "Open Gardens"? While we were away staying with friends, the Lady of the House and I had great fun visiting one of these events.

What happens is every homeowner who chooses to participate opens their garden to the public. It was fascinating exploring the various plots – small and large, charming, quirky and some definitely a work in progress!

We visitors thoroughly enjoyed our day, as did the owners, who were giving tips and receiving admiration in pretty much equal measure!

And, of course, the event was hailed as a great success by the local charities who benefited from the generous sum raised from donations.

We thought it was a blooming good idea!

Tuesday — **June 2**

THE film actress Audrey Hepburn made many good friends during her career, both in the studio and among the fans who wrote asking for tips on how to break into show business.

Audrey, like all professional thespians, used to reply with a sensible tip or two, and would remind the would-be stars that good luck was needed in addition to acting talent.

Then, in a friendly aside, she would add this neat little postscript.

"Never pay attention to the people who say your ambition to become a star is IMpossible. Just ask them to look more closely – even the word itself now says 'I'm possible'!"

Wednesday — **June 3**

IT is comforting to know that everyone makes mistakes in life. Horace said, "Mistakes are their own instructors."

Actress Mary Pickford, who endured many troubles in her life, said, "If you have made mistakes, there is always another chance for you. You may have a fresh start any moment you choose, for this thing we call failure is not the falling down but the staying down."

So pick yourself up from that low point and grab that second chance! Success is in your own hands.

Thursday — **June 4**

THERE'S no such thing as boring,
Or common or mundane,
And if you truly think so,
It's time to think again!
For everything around you
Holds powers to entrance,
Just choose to stop and notice –
Your life you'll much enhance.
So keep your mind wide open,
It's easy once you start,
For even in a cobweb
You'll find a work of art!

Margaret Ingall.

Friday — **June 5**

THE trees of the garden should bear more fruit than the trees of the forest," wrote Christopher Love, a Welsh preacher. I supposed that must be because the trees of the garden are loved and cared for. Now if we can lovingly encourage such growth in trees, what might we do with family and friends? And what difference might we make to the world if we gently expanded our garden?

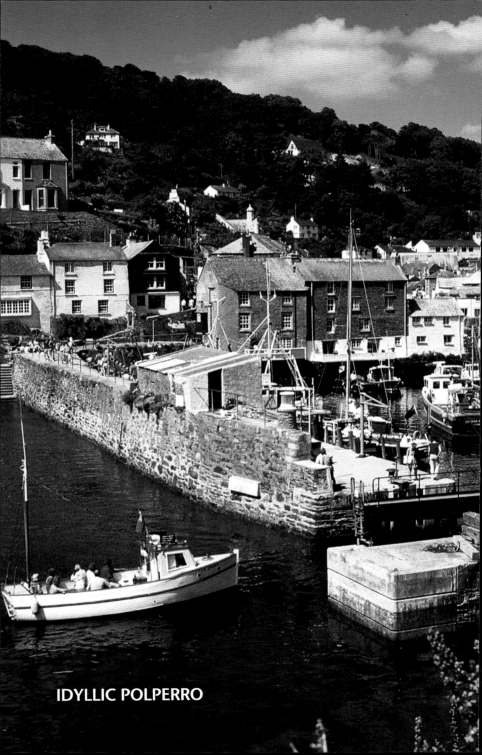

IDYLLIC POLPERRO

Saturday — **June 6**

SEAN COVEY writes motivational books for young people. He says, "We become what we repeatedly do." In other words, we can train ourselves. So, by doing a good deed every day, by helping the needy, by involving ourselves in prayer, or whatever our personal aim might be, we can become the kind of person we want to be – hopefully a better person. So let's do good repeatedly and feel the difference!

Sunday — **June 7**

SAM was smiling as he showed me a postcard he'd received, simply bearing the words "Ecclesiastes 11:7".

"It's from Ben and Lucy," he said. "They're on holiday in Guernsey. They had a rotten time when the rain flooded our street last year, but they were always ready to help out. I'm really glad they're having good weather and time to enjoy it."

I think we all benefit from some kind of break from everyday life, even if that doesn't include the drama of floods. So, even if an actual holiday can't be managed, let's at least try to allow ourselves to catch that moment of sunlight.

Oh, yes, and what does Ecclesiastes 11:7 have to say?

"Truly the light is sweet, and a pleasant thing it is for the eyes to behold the sun."

Monday — **June 8**

TALK about being careful what you wish for!" Joanne exclaimed. "I've just been reading about someone who won a million pounds and it caused no end of problems – fighting in the family . . . but here's also a story about a man who was devastated when he lost his job as a manager, and then discovered he was much happier as a musician!"

This put me in mind of something said by Richard Bach: "There's no disaster that can't become a blessing, and no blessing that can't become a disaster."

Tuesday — **June 9**

BILL was telling me about a domino topple that he'd been watching on television.

"You should have seen it, Francis," he said. "It was amazing how the tipping over of just one domino led to a whole chain of marvellous effects!"

It certainly did sound impressive, but Brazilian writer and lyricist Paulo Coelho writes of a different domino effect which is even more exciting.

"When we love, we always strive to become better than we are. When we strive to become better than we are, everything around us becomes better, too."

Now that's a domino effect we can all try!

Wednesday — **June 10**

TODAY I came across a lovely little quote that had me nodding in agreement even as I read it.

"The impossible is only the untried."

Thursday — **June 11**

ARTUR SCHNABEL was one of the most respected classical pianists of the 20th century. While others praised his ability, he tended to downplay it a little.

"The notes I handle no better than many pianists," he said. "But the pauses between the notes . . . that is where the art resides."

If our lives were musical scores then many of the notes would be the same no matter who was playing: work, relationships, commuting, paying the bills. But the pauses – ah, those are the spaces where we make our lives unique by taking time for appreciation, love, wonder, listening, doing all the things we don't have to do.

Let's make the most of our pauses, and turn life into a classical composition.

Friday — June 12

ANOTHER birthday! Have you noticed how, as we grow older, these special days seem to creep up on us quite stealthily?

Nevertheless, the Lady of the House was pleased with all the birthday greetings she received. Enclosed in one of the cards was a little present – a pretty bookmark.

"Another bookmark!" I exclaimed with a smile, though I know how much she likes them.

"Yes," she replied. "But look at this, Francis. My friend must have known how I would be feeling today!"

The message on the bookmark read, *Don't count the years, count the blessings.* I felt those were very wise words. When my next birthday arrives I shall certainly keep that advice in mind.

And I might even borrow the bookmark!

Saturday — June 13

IT'S amazing," Mick said to me the other day, "just how much good can come from change. Although," he added with a smile, "I admit that it rarely seems good when it's actually happening."

I agree with Mick's observation. Changes in our life can very often appear to be threatening, but without change life would surely have little meaning.

As C.S. Lewis observed, "It may be hard for an egg to turn into a bird, but it would be a jolly sight harder for it to learn to fly while remaining an egg. We are like eggs at present. And you cannot go on indefinitely being just an ordinary, decent egg. We must be hatched or go bad."

And who would choose to become a bad egg if they had the chance to soar?

Sunday — **June 14**

IT may have been the sunny day with its clear blue sky that prompted the Lady of the House to ask, "What's the shortest prayer, Francis?" I didn't know! But later I remembered the words of Ralph Waldo Emerson:

For flowers that bloom about our feet,
For tender grass so fresh and sweet,
For all things fair we hear or see,
Father in heaven, we thank thee.
For this new morning with its light,
For rest and shelter of the night,
For health and food, for love and friends,
For everything thy goodness sends,
Father in heaven, we thank thee.

Brevity can be a fine thing, but thanking God can be a life-long prayer.

Monday — **June 15**

HENRY'S wealthy father thought him the dullest of his sons so, instead of wasting money on a good education, sent him to work for a friend in South Africa. Henry loved it. He learned to converse with the Zulus and discovered their folklore. This inspired him to write. The result was a string of novels, including "King Solomon's Mines" and "Allan Quatermain". H. Rider Haggard, the "dull boy" from Norfolk, gave us some of the most exciting adventure stories ever written.

Tuesday — **June 16**

SOMETIMES it's easy to get caught up in the busyness of life and forget what matters most. Recently, I was gently reminded when I came across these lovely words:

"In the comfort of what's familiar and in the faces of those we love, we own all the treasures of life."

SEEKING SHELTER

Wednesday — **June 17**

CLARA SCHUMANN had a 60-year career as a classical pianist, during which time she encouraged Brahms in his compositions and her talent was admired by Liszt and Chopin. She once said, "My imagination can picture no fairer happiness than to continue living for art."

We can all find that level of happiness if we first find something to live for that means as much to us as music did to Clara Schumann. Then, having found it, we can raise our happiness to the level of an art!

Thursday — **June 18**

HAVE you heard of the idea of six degrees of separation? It's the theory that everyone in the world can be connected to each other through a chain of friends that has no more than six other people. I'd love to believe it's true. The more we all realise we have much in common, then perhaps the less likely we will be to fall out. And that surely can't be a bad thing!

Friday — **June 19**

THESE days I prefer to do my mountaineering from the comfort of an armchair with a good book in hand. That's how I followed Erik Weihenmayer up Mount McKinlay, the highest peak in North America. It was a mighty challenge – especially since Erik is blind! Understandably, he was often frustrated – in fact, frustration became his biggest obstacle until he found a way to deal with it.

"I made a promise to myself," he wrote, "that the things I couldn't do – and there were many – I would let go, but the things I could do – and there were also many – I would learn to do well."

Good advice, and not just for blind mountaineers, but for the rest of us, as well!

Saturday — June 20

THE farmer had a problem with his tiny dog named Minnie. She was so small she could slip in and out of the cat flap on the farmhouse door! Then he discovered she had taken to nipping down rabbit holes and was likely to become trapped.

He appealed to a friend who was very fond of dogs and already had a greyhound, a gentle giant named Bran. So the little dog went off to her new home where there was a large garden, but no cat flaps or rabbit holes.

Bran was a little doubtful at first when he met the new arrival, but they soon settled down together. They make a strange pair when out for a walk, but they have learned to live in harmony and seem quite contented.

This little story set me thinking how we humans ought to be more adaptable and understanding of each other. In spite of our differences, we need to go forward, side by side, and create a little harmony in the world and in our lives. A lesson we can all learn from Minnie and Bran!

Sunday — June 21

BETH, a teacher, was talking about helping the children learn how to weigh and measure various commodities.

"They always prefer calculating the easiest things." She smiled. "But I suppose that's just human nature."

I'm sure she's right, which is why we so often tend to measure people's success only in terms of money or possessions, ignoring other far greater, but less tangible, qualities.

That's why I'm so fond of Johnson Oatman's words for the hymn "Count Your Blessings".

When you look at others with their lands and gold,
Think that Christ has promised you his wealth untold,
Count your many blessings wealth can never buy:
Your reward in heaven nor your home on high.

Monday — **June 22**

RUSH, rush, rush. Sometimes it seems our world is so busy that no-one has time to pause and listen to one another, to offer help, encouragement, or even a cheering remark. So let's remember the words of Sylvia Rossetti, who said, "Genuine kindness is no ordinary act, but a gift of rare beauty".

Who wouldn't want to spare a moment to offer such a gift?

Tuesday — **June 23**

I WISH you summer mornings
With birdsong on the breeze,
And summer nights of quiet peace
With moonlight through the trees.
I wish you autumn splendour
With russet, red and gold,
A harvest of your very own
As memories unfold.

I wish you sweet contentment
As winter brings a chill,
The comfort of your hearth and home
And love to warm you still.
I wish you springtime glory
As earth awakes anew,
May every season of the year
Hold happiness for you.

Iris Hesselden.

Wednesday — **June 24**

WHAT is your definition of a miracle? Buddhist monk Thích Nhất Hạnh says: "People usually consider walking on water or in thin air a miracle. But I think the real miracle is not to walk either on water or in thin air, but to walk on earth. Every day we are engaged in a miracle which we don't even recognise: a blue sky, white clouds, green leaves, the black, curious eyes of a child – our own two eyes. All is a miracle."

Thursday — **June 25**

WHEN the great storyteller, Hans Christian Andersen, wrote, "Just living is not enough. One must have sunshine, freedom and a little flower", he was speaking in the voice of a butterfly.

Now butterflies have a practical use for flowers, but for the rest of us, freedom and sunshine might be looked on as necessities, but a little flower hardly qualifies. But it's having space for some unnecessary beauty that makes life more than just an existence. That's what makes it worth living.

If you don't have a little flower in your life today, might I suggest you take the butterfly's advice?

Friday — **June 26**

YOU might store food in plastic containers; you might store money in the bank; you, doubtless, store your clothes in a wardrobe or a chest of drawers or some such. But what about the more intangible things? Is it even possible to store them?

In his Sacrament of Common Life, John S. Hoyland tells us it is possible. "A home," he says, "is a treasury of God, wherein purity, beauty and joy are stored for His purpose."

Saturday — **June 27**

STANDING outside the greengrocer's, Sheila was busily scanning the piece of paper in her hand.

"Hello, Francis." She waved. "I'm just checking my list – otherwise I'd end up going home without half the stuff I need."

Lists are great when there are things we need to remember. But, as American broadcaster Bernard Meltzer pointed out, there are times when we actually do better to forget.

"Blessed are those who give without remembering," he observed. "And blessed are those who take without forgetting."

Sunday — **June 28**

I TELL you, Francis, it was scary!" But Jane was smiling as she described her coach trip in Italy, and a route which had followed many hairpin bends round some very steep drops.

"I found myself clutching the arm-rest and holding my breath at every turn," she continued. "And then, I suddenly realised that however alarmed I was, the driver knew what he was doing. So I decided just to relax and enjoy. And it worked!"

What a sensible attitude. And Jane's story is worth recalling whenever our own lives feel out of control. Remember – there is a Driver who knows exactly what He's doing!

Monday — **June 29**

T ED is well known in our area for his willingness to help others, and is often praised for his kindness. "Kind?" he'll say. "I don't see it as such. You see, I end up just as happy as the people I help."

A. Neilen said, "If you have not often felt the joy of doing a kind act, you have neglected much, and most of all yourself."

Words to remember, next time we hesitate to volunteer!

Tuesday — **June 30**

W HEN new sea defences were put in place along Saltcoats shore, a line of granite boulders was laid to dissipate the force of the waves before they hit the sea-wall. No-one would have predicted that anything would have taken root in the space between the boulders and the wall. As the Lady of the House and I walked past what should have been bare granite we saw a fine display of pink and white flowers.

"Two excellent ways to live," my sweetheart murmured thoughtfully. "Be the strength that allows beauty to flower – or be the beauty which makes the strength worthwhile."

July

SIR HUMPHREY DAVY was given a baronetcy for his scientific work, and his Davy lamp has saved the lives of many miners. He didn't reach such exalted status without making mistakes along the way, though. "The most important of my discoveries," he wrote, "have been suggested to me by my failures."

On a lighter note, Lionel Jeffries, in the film "Chitty Chitty Bang Bang", sang, "From the ashes of disaster grow the roses of success."

So next time things go wrong, let's take their tip – wait a bit, and see what new wonder grows from the ashes.

A TRUE friend has a generous heart,
A flair for knowing what to say,
Is someone you can call upon
At any hour of night or day.
Is someone thoughtful, caring, warm,
Who's journeyed often by your side,
Who's shared your triumphs, yet remained
A comfort in the times you've cried.

Is one with whom you'll laugh for hours,
And as you reminisce, you'll find
That countless memories are shared,
So tightly are your lives entwined.
And if you're blessed with such a friend
Who's dearly loved and always true,
Then there's no doubt they, too, possess
A true and loving friend in you.

Emma Canning.

July

Wednesday — July 1

SIR HUMPHREY DAVY was given a baronetcy for his scientific work, and his Davy lamp has saved the lives of many miners. He didn't reach such exalted status without making mistakes along the way, though. "The most important of my discoveries," he wrote, "have been suggested to me by my failures."

On a lighter note, Lionel Jeffries, in the film "Chitty Chitty Bang Bang", sang, "From the ashes of disaster grow the roses of success."

So next time things go wrong, let's take their tip – wait a bit, and see what new wonder grows from the ashes.

Thursday — July 2

A TRUE friend has a generous heart,
A flair for knowing what to say,
Is someone you can call upon
At any hour of night or day.
Is someone thoughtful, caring, warm,
Who's journeyed often by your side,
Who's shared your triumphs, yet remained
A comfort in the times you've cried.

Is one with whom you'll laugh for hours,
And as you reminisce, you'll find
That countless memories are shared,
So tightly are your lives entwined.
And if you're blessed with such a friend
Who's dearly loved and always true,
Then there's no doubt they, too, possess
A true and loving friend in you.

Emma Canning.

Friday — July 3

JUST after the end of the American Civil War President Lincoln requested that a band treat him to a rendition of "Dixie", the anthem of the South, declaring it was one of the best tunes he had ever heard.

There and then that wise gentleman showed the world people could be opponents for many reasons, but they shouldn't let the differences blind them to each other's good points – of which, no matter the dispute, there are usually many!

Saturday — July 4

YOU know the kind of people who have exactly the same approach to good times and bad times? Well, our friend Mary surprised me by insisting she wasn't one of them.

"I do have a different approach to the different circumstances," Mary told me, "but it's only one letter of a difference."

She took pity on my confused expression and explained.

"Well, I try to be graceful in the bad times . . . and grateful in the good."

Sunday — July 5

THE major ports may have been smoky places in the days of Sir Francis Drake. After all, Plymouth, Portsmouth and the rest would have depended on coal, wood and oil for cooking, heating and industry.

He could have been referring to leaving such pollution behind when he wrote, "Losing sight of land, we shall find the stars." But actually he meant that God never takes us beyond our known limits without providing new guidance when we get there.

A comforting thought for the fabled sailor – and for each of us on our personal voyage.

A BIT OF "ME" TIME!

Monday — July 6

THE actor Alan Rickman was once asked which piece of art he would most like to own. He told of the time he had seen Michelangelo's Madonna and Child in Bruges. But if he owned it, he explained, then other people would have to settle for seeing it in pictures. So, he would rather not own it. He would rather it was shared.

From a simple kindness, to a work of art, to the grandeur of nature, I have to agree. Beauty is made to be shared, and the act of sharing often seems to make it even more beautiful!

Tuesday — July 7

ONE of Harry's shrubs had fallen victim to an over-exuberant dog. A V-shaped branch near the bottom had split almost completely off. But he reckoned the sap was still flowing and he could save it. So, with pliers, wire and a lot of tender care he secured the fallen branch to another.

"St Francis would have approved, you know," he said. "He said, 'We are called to heal wounds. To unite what has fallen apart'." He smiled at his shrub. "I reckon that's what I did there."

Now, if only we could take St Francis's advice and Harry's gardening tip out into the rest of the world.

Wednesday — July 8

WHEN I was younger," Hector said, "people kept telling me how good I was at making little ornaments out of wood, and now I rather wish they hadn't.

"You see," he explained, "I became so accustomed to easy success that it was a long time before I was brave enough to try making a violin. And now it's what I love doing most."

Michelangelo said, "The greatest danger for most of us lies not in setting our aim too high and falling short, but in setting our aim too low, and achieving our mark."

For if we reach high, we may just make beautiful music.

Thursday — **July 9**

*H*E is the kaleidoscope of the rainbow,
    The chuckle of a stream,
The lark's glad call, the lily's perfume.
He is the bud on the branch,
The rich gleam of the fox's fur,
The shy gaze of a fawn,
The small cloud caught in a crate of trees.
He is the gold that crowns the daffodils,
The whisper in the wind, the song in the rain,
The story of the seasons.
He is life and love, the beginning and the end,
An hour, a day, an eternity.
                    Rachel Wallace-Oberle.

Friday — **July 10**

I CAN'T deny it's been hard to continue painting," Gerry said, "but it would have been much harder to give up." He was showing me round his exhibition of watercolours, beautifully executed local landscapes. My admiration was deepened by the knowledge of his debilitating health problems.

French poet Jean de La Fontaine said, "Mankind is so made that when anything fires the soul, impossibilities vanish."

I think he must have known someone just like Gerry!

Saturday — **July 11**

TALLULAH BANKHEAD once quipped, "Nobody can be exactly like me. Sometimes even I had trouble doing it!"

We are all unique. Being you, one of a kind, probably doesn't take much effort. It's a natural talent, if you like. But being the best "you" you can be – now that takes a lot of effort. The end result, however, will be a performance fit to grace any silver screen!

Sunday — July 12

CONNIE runs an internet site where local people can give away stuff they don't need any more. She knows that a lot of the things that take up space in garages or attic could be put to good use. And, besides, the council often charge to have these things uplifted.

"But the most wonderful thing is that the people who get the most out of it are usually those giving things away."

Give, and it will be given to you. A good measure, pressed down, shaken together and running over, will be poured into your lap. For with the measure you use, it will be measured to you. Luke 6:38.

Monday — July 13

THERE'S a road in Stevenston called Darg Street. "Darg" means day's work, or the amount of coal dug in a shift. Miners were known to include it in their prayers. "Thank you for our daily bread and thank you for our darg."

Working days are very different now, but the idea of having a purpose is still an important one. Whether your day is helping others, tapping at a keyboard, teaching, or raising the children, remember to give thanks for your daily darg – and be glad it doesn't involve shifting tons of coal!

Tuesday — July 14

IT'S funny," Sarah said, "how our feelings about birthdays change as we go through life. I share a birthday with my little granddaughter, who's always eager for her big day to arrive. I'd have said my feelings were exactly the opposite!

"But I discovered some words by Helen Hayes which cheered me up. She said, 'The best way to adjust – no, ignore – most of the negative thoughts about ageing is to say to yourself, "I am still the very same person I have been all my adult life".' "

Yes. Not only encouraging – it's true!

TAKING A BREAK

Wednesday — **July 15**

I REMEMBER (across the centuries, as it sometimes seems) a teacher saying, "If you have any questions, class, ask me. If I don't know the answer I'll ask the class. If they don't know the answer, why then, we shall embark upon an adventure of discovery!"

Whether you be a teacher, a parent, or an educator of any kind, if you would teach children anything first teach them the wonder and excitement of learning!

Thursday — **July 16**

ARE you are familiar with the diaries of Nella Last? She began writing at the start of World War II, as part of the Mass Observation project.

It is often said that writers reveal more of themselves than they realise, and in Nella Last's case, what a joy it is to get to know her. In a post-war entry of a journey to visit her son in Ireland, she says she was "a lucky traveller" as she so often found herself sitting next to "nice people".

I rather think Nella herself brought out the best in people. It's a great gift, and one that's worth cultivating.

In fact, I'll just make a note of that in my diary!

Friday — **July 17**

IT was praised by no less a person than four-times Prime Minister William Gladstone.

"If you are cold," he wrote, "it will warm you. If you are too heated it will cool you. If you are depressed it will cheer you. If you are excited it will calm you."

And might I add that two of them will bring two separate people closer.

What is this wonderful thing? Why, it's tea! Who knew a dear old cuppa could do so much?

Saturday — **July 18**

IN the children's book "Charlotte's Web", the spider of the title does all she can to save a piglet called Wilbur. Eventually, thanks to her efforts, Wilbur becomes a famous prize pig and his life is guaranteed to be long and comfortable.

At one point he asks his companion, "Why did you do all this for me? I don't deserve it. I've never done anything for you." And Charlotte replies, "You have been my friend. That in itself is a tremendous thing."

Anyone who has ever had a friend will know exactly what she meant.

Sunday — **July 19**

WHENEVER I'm tempted to feel gloomy about the human race, it's strange how often I come across something which restores all my hope.

One such is the account of Horatio and Anna Spafford. Living in 19th-century America, they were a devout Christian couple, parents of five, and active in the abolitionist movement. Tragedy struck when their only son died, aged four, of scarlet fever. Then their finances were severely struck by the Great Chicago Fire, but a far greater heartbreak awaited when their four remaining children were drowned in a shipwreck.

Despite the devastation, their Christian trust stayed sure, and on a later voyage sailing close to the site of the disaster, Horatio wrote a hymn, "It Is Well With My Soul", that has brought comfort to a great many other sad hearts:

When peace, like a river, attendeth my way
When sorrows like sea billows roll;
Whatever my lot, thou hast taught me to say
It is well, it is well with my soul.

Beautiful words from a man whose faith must inspire us all.

Monday — **July 20**

SPARKLING season, scorching sand,
Sheltered shallows, sunspot scanned;
Sea so sultry – signals storm,
Swimmers scatter – safety swarm!

Showers sharpen, stinging spray,
Swift, staccato soaking stay;
Streaming shingle, spreading strong,
Summer's serenading song!
                                Elizabeth Gozney.

Tuesday — **July 21**

THE poet Robert Southey told a story of a Spaniard who always put on his glasses to eat cherries. Why? Because that way he got to see how good they looked as well as taste how delicious they were. He was making the most of those cherries!

"In like manner," Southey wrote, "I pack my troubles in as small a package as I can – and make the most of my enjoyments!"

Wednesday — **July 22**

THE Lady of the House was delighted with the gift she received from our young friend, Katie. It wasn't anything large or expensive – just a packet of her favourite sweets.

"I just saw it and thought of you. It's an N.S.R. gift."

We both looked puzzled. With a smile she explained, "No Special Reason! That is what it is."

What a lovely idea – and how uplifting to receive something unexpectedly. If you know someone who is in need of a little sunshine in their life, you could offer a single flower or a bar of chocolate. It doesn't have to be expensive. Just knowing that they were in your thoughts will be enough to give them a lift for the rest of the day!

Thursday — **July 23**

IT was a bad blow when Paul found he was being made redundant, and for a while he was lost, uncertain what to do next.

"I can remember the exact point when I came to a decision," he said. "I'd gone up to the little wood at the top of the hill. It's always such a peaceful place, and as I sat there, I realised the answer was all around me. I'd always enjoyed painting landscapes, so why not take the opportunity to try making it into a career? Nowadays, although my income is smaller, my job satisfaction has never been so great."

It was writer Hermann Hesse who wrote, "Trees are sanctuaries. Whoever knows how to speak to them, whoever knows how to listen to them, can learn the truth."

I suspect that applies to most of nature's quiet places. All we need is a little patience.

Friday — **July 24**

THE phrase, "You can't choose your family," is often used as a complaint or muttered in a sigh of frustration, but Archbishop Desmond Tutu had an altogether more positive take on the subject.

"You don't choose your family," he reminded us. "They are God's gift to you – as you are to them."

Saturday — **July 25**

I HAVE heard it said (and I believe it) that smiling, even when you don't feel like it, will make you feel happier.
Art Linkletter, the Canadian TV and radio personality, took that thought just a little further.

"Just smiling," he said, "goes a long way toward making you feel better about life. And when you feel better about life – your life is better!"

Sunday — **July 26**

JOAN was showing me some photos that she'd taken during a recent holiday in Spain.

"One thing that I discovered, Francis," she informed me, "is that in Spain the term 'patio' doesn't just describe a flat area outside a back door. Instead it denotes a quiet courtyard in the middle of a busy building, away from heat and noise, and often beautifully decorated with flowers, ferns, or a fountain."

How delightful that sounds. And though I don't imagine many of us can boast such a patio, there's nothing to stop us cultivating such a place in our hearts and minds; a calm and quiet space in which to retreat and refresh our spirits.

Worth a try, don't you think?

Monday — **July 27**

THERE'S a notice at a viewpoint looking out over the Grand Canyon. It explains in detail all the interesting features to be seen and the geology. But, beside that, is a simpler sign. It says, *For one minute, don't read, don't talk, no photos, just look . . . and see.*

For all the wonders of the world, abroad or in your garden, once in a lifetime or every day, I think that is "grand" advice.

Tuesday — **July 28**

COULD you and I improve on John Keats, the poet? In "Bright Star" he wrote, "I almost wish we were butterflies and liv'd but three summer days – three such days with you I could fill with more delight than fifty common years could ever contain."

Now, how could we improve on such a beautiful sentiment? By not settling for such things as "common years", but living our days delightfully and making all, or as many as possible, "butterfly days".

Wednesday — July 29

YESTERDAY I went to a coffee morning being held to celebrate the anniversary of a group which came into being almost by accident. Concerned at the state of the local playground, a collection of residents got together to make sure it was properly maintained.

That original group grew in numbers, began to take on new community projects and, 10 years later, is still going strong.

As I took the chance to offer them my own congratulations, I was given a smiling reply in the form of a quote from Henry Ford: "Coming together is a beginning. Keeping together is progress. Working together is success."

And best of all, a success you can share with others!

Thursday — July 30

HAVE you heard of "reverse graffiti"? Instead of using spray paint on walls, some more imaginative artists are finding grubby buildings in industrial areas and cleaning them up by painting beautiful landscapes or tropical vistas on to them!

What a shame we can't do that with the less attractive parts of our lives. But perhaps we can. And the best kind of cleaning solution to use? Forgiveness.

Friday — July 31

TO a child, the wisest person in the whole wide world is usually Mummy, Daddy or perhaps Teacher. All of those would be good candidates for the title, but I think the outright winner for the "Fount Of All Knowledge" award will usually be a grandparent!

And why is that? Is it because, having lived longer, they have learned more? Or is it, as Charles Dickens wrote, that "a loving heart is the truest wisdom"? And nobody loves like Grandma or Grandpa!

August

Saturday — August 1

WE'VE had a guest for a week," John told me. "My daughter's penfriend from France has been staying with us. Our Zoe certainly enjoyed it, but it was a good experience for the whole family. Taking Monique out and about made us see our locality with new eyes, and appreciate just how interesting our area is."

"I can understand that," the Lady of the House agreed when I told her. "It's so easy to take for granted the area in which you live, especially if you've been there for some time. So let's make a pact, Francis – every time we go for a walk we'll try to look around us as if we were showing a foreign visitor around."

What else could I reply except, "*Mais oui!*"

Sunday — August 2

THE daughter of a business dynasty held a Bible study group at her house. Serving the most elegant of afternoon teas on the finest of bone china, she quietly said, "Only the best. Only the best for Him."

One who was there assured me the woman's delight didn't come from the quality of the food, or the cost of the crockery – it came from offering God the best she had to give.

And we don't need to be heirs or heiresses to a fortune to do that. Each of us, no matter our situation, can offer the Lord our best.

And, come to think of it, we are all heirs and heiresses – to the Kingdom of Heaven.

VIBRANT DAHLIAS

Monday — **August 3**

WHEN I left college," David said, "I thought I knew everything about everything. It gave me the confidence to get a good job, but I can't say it helped me work with other people, or do anything to make the world a better place."

I suspect he need not have worried too much, for David has for many years been a most useful and well-liked member of his community. All the same, I knew what he meant.

To quote Sandra Carey: "Never mistake knowledge for wisdom, for one helps you make a living, the other helps you make a life."

May all our lives be enriched by wisdom – for the great thing is that it's never too late to acquire it.

Tuesday — **August 4**

I LIKE this advice from the Burmese pro-democracy leader Aung San Suu Kyi – "If you're feeling helpless," she wrote, "help someone."

A nice reminder that while we might occasionally be unable to alter our own circumstances, we can usually improve someone else's. And in making other people's lives better, we almost inevitably help improve our own.

Wednesday — **August 5**

INSTRUCTIONS! Being a man I rarely read them. (And when I do read them I rarely understand them!)

They should be simple, to the point and leave you feeling that you will be better off for following them. Which is why I liked these "Instructions For Living" by the poet Mary Oliver:

"Pay attention.
Be astonished.
Tell about it."

Thursday — **August 6**

IT'S well known that Lewis Carroll wrote "Alice's Adventures In Wonderland" for Alice Liddell, the daughter of friends. What's less well known is that before he showed the story to Alice, he read it to the children of fellow writer George MacDonald.

Carroll never intended the book to be published, but the applause and admiration of the MacDonald children convinced him to show it to a publisher – who snapped it up!

And so one of the greatest children's stories ever came to be a gift to the world. Isn't it amazing – or should I say "Wonder"-ful – what a little appreciation can do?

Friday — **August 7**

MARY was in a bit of a reverie when I walked over to her. She was gazing into the primary school playground.

"Do you know what's wonderful about children?" she asked, after she recovered from the shock of my hand on her shoulder. "They don't need a reason to be happy. Most grown-ups need a reason, and those reasons can go away. But if we could find the secret of being happy for no reason, like these little ones, then happiness could never be taken away from us."

I admit I often need reasons to be happy – and one of them is Mary!

Saturday — **August 8**

MY heart pounds and the tears stream from my eyes and my emotions and my joys are too much to bear." The great composer Giuseppe Verdi was describing how he sometimes felt when alone with his music. There are countless aspects of the world with the ability to lift our hearts like this.

What would make that kind of difference to you?

Sunday — **August 9**

DO you ever feel you would like to do a great work for God? Imagine being the Scottish minister asked to vacate his parish because he'd failed to bring any new converts to the church. Actually, he did have one convert, wee Bobby Moffat, but, as a child, he didn't count.

Bobby Moffat did count, though. As an African missionary he earned the respect of Parliament and the King. He later became David Livingstone's father-in-law.

God doesn't necessarily want great works done in his name. He wants us to speak words of love, do small kindnesses, tell someone the Good News.

He will take those little offerings and make them great!

Monday — **August 10**

HOW often have you heard someone say, "Oh, dear, another birthday?" I have even heard "I'm not having any more birthdays – that's it!" asserted more than once!

I came across the following in a little birthday book.

"In the 365 days since your last birthday you have become wiser without even trying. Wisdom is one of the nicest gifts of all, because in order to acquire it, all you have to do is live. Wisdom is a keepsake you accumulate every year."

So next time you have a birthday, don't think how old you are, but how wise you have become!

Tuesday — **August 11**

IT'S only a drop in the ocean," you sometimes hear folk say,
"Why bother even trying? Give up – just walk away."
Such words must surely dampen each spirit and each heart,
And sometimes stop us trying before we even start.
But do not get discouraged; remember – here's the key:
Enough drops in the ocean can make a mighty sea!
Margaret Ingall.

Wednesday — **August 12**

THE American novelist Nathaniel Hawthorne once wrote a book of essays on his time in England. He had hoped to use his observations as background for a work of fiction but "the present, the immediate, and the actual proved too potent." The richness and variety of real life made fiction seem temporarily uninteresting by comparison.

Now, I like a good novel as much as anyone, but if we want to be blown away by wonder let's look beyond imagination and pay closer attention to the real world; to "the present, the immediate and the actual."

Thursday — **August 13**

YOU can't improve on Paradise, I'm sure of that. But I would suggest that paradise with a small "p" might be made better. The word comes from an ancient Indo-European language and means a walled garden. So, how do you improve on a walled garden? Let people in. Like all blessings it will be increased by sharing it.

Now, we don't all have walled gardens, but if you have a place that comforts your soul or makes your heart sing share it with a friend. And you will have improved paradise!

Friday — **August 14**

AS I walked into the shopping mall the door slid open in front of me. People were talking on mobile phones or using them to access information which might have been half a world away. It all reminded me of Star Trek!

When the series began in 1966, automatic doors and "communicators" were very much the fiction part of science fiction. But now they are real. As the poet William Blake said, "What is now proved was once only imagined."

With that in mind, perhaps we should imagine a world of peace and plenty. Stranger things have happened!

Saturday — **August 15**

THE days of class division are long behind us, but in 1932 things were a little different. The newspaper from that year told a story of "a man of the tramp class" who saved a child from drowning.

The meaning might be slightly different, but I like to think the story showed that we can walk the roads, work in offices, occupy whatever station in life, but when we put others before ourselves that's when we show the kind of class that really matters.

Sunday — **August 16**

MANY a time I have stood gazing in awe at the view from a hilltop or at the sun setting over the sea. On a few occasions I have tried to preserve those moments in photos, but they rarely do them justice.

Being a naturalist and living in Switzerland, Conrad Gesner (who lived in the 16th century) would have been familiar with that feeling. He suggested this method of remembering.

"Best of all," he wrote, "preserve everything in a pure, still heart, and let there be for every pulse a thanksgiving, and for every breath a song."

A method that might also be applied to blessings of every kind.

Monday — **August 17**

SURELY you are all of you, and I am all of me! But Harry Emerson Fosdick, the 20th-century clergyman, might well have disagreed with my assumption. And, having heard his explanation, I might well have disagreed with myself!

"No man," he wrote, "is the whole of himself. His friends are the rest of him!"

Tuesday — **August 18**

*I*T'S always fun to choose a gift,
A present for a child,
To wander round the shelves of toys,
By all their joys beguiled.
Some building bricks? A teddy bear?
A big red bouncing ball?
Yet though such things entice our eye,
One gift still beats them all:
It's Time that children relish most,
It's Time, to talk and play,
To know that someone's listening, too,
And hearing all they say.
And though we cannot wrap it up
With ribbons or a bow,
It's Time they'll treasure all their life,
And helps them truly grow.

Margaret Ingall.

Wednesday — **August 19**

A CERTAIN writer from times gone past published a book called "The Friendly Year". In his introduction he said he could just as easily have written a book about the unfriendly people and incidents he had encountered in the previous year – if he could remember them. His chosen disposition was such that the good stayed with him while the other stuff fell behind.

What a wonderful way to see the world, and one which we might benefit from trying to copy.

Oh, and did I mention that the book was published in 1940? The previous year had seen the beginning of World War II, a sad fact that didn't rate a mention when compared with all the good deeds he had seen and the friendly people he had met.

Thursday — **August 20**

THERE'S a fine road between Bremhill and Langley Burrell in Wiltshire, but alongside it runs a raised walkway atop 64 small brick arches. The walkway was a gift to the future from Maud Heath, a widow who, in the 15th century, used to take her eggs to market along that route.

She walked along a flood plain and often became stuck in the boggy ground. When she retired, after years of struggling with the mud, she invested some of her savings in a raised walkway for the women who still walked that way.

The charity that hatched from Maud Heath's eggs (and her generosity of spirit) still preserves the walkway today.

Friday — **August 21**

A CHINESE king in ancient times had a motto inscribed on his bath. It said, "If you would one day renovate yourself, do so from day to day. Yea, let there be daily renovation." In other words, if you would be a better person some day – start today!

I still thought it was a strange place to keep a motto. But, of course, if he had a daily bath he could wash away a bad habit each day!

Saturday — **August 22**

THEY say we never part from friends, and that, I'm sure, is so,
For friends remain a part of us wherever we may go.
A photograph, a recipe, an old familiar view,
So often brings fond thoughts to mind of folk that we once knew.
For though life's changes sometimes mean our paths may cross no more,
Our friends remain within our hearts, for ever safe and sure.

                                        Margaret Ingall.

Sunday — **August 23**

I HADN'T thought Mary was late for our countryside rendezvous, but she apologised anyway.

"On my way," she explained, "I detected the most beautiful scent and I just had to search out the blossom responsible and tell it thank you." She acquired a faraway look in her eye. "Imagine if we lived our lives like that," she said.

"Ha!" I retorted. "We'd never get anything done."

"We'd get different things done," Mary said softly. "And our thank yous would be never ending."

Monday — **August 24**

THE American President James Garfield once offered this opinion: "There are men and women who make the world better just by being the kind of people they are. They have the gift of kindness or courage or loyalty or integrity. It really matters very little whether they are behind the wheel of a truck or running a business or bringing up a family. They teach the truth by living it."

To that I offer an opinion of my own – you will know someone who is that kind of person, if only you care to look around for them. Better still, you may be that person!

Tuesday — **August 25**

PETS, children, parents, a spouse, friends, people we may have helped, those who quietly remove obstacles from our way, the chance occurrence that seems ordained . . .

Just a few of the things that came to mind when I read the artist Vincent Van Gogh's opinion of love. He described it as, "something eternal; the aspect may change, but not the essence."

It seems that if we don't always expect it to look the same we can always expect to find it!

Wednesday — **August 26**

THE writers of the inspirational "Chicken Soup For The Soul" books had a hard time getting anyone to publish them. Then a friend said, "If you take five swings at a tree with an axe each day, then it doesn't matter how big that tree is, it will eventually come down!"

So they set themselves the target of calling five radio stations a day to try to get interviews, or sending copies to five different editors. Eventually, they got a publishing deal and the books have sold over a hundred million copies. It's a great lesson in perseverance paying off – and all for only five swings a day!

Thursday — **August 27**

ACCORDING to science, worlds are formed by the cooling of cosmic "debris" around a star. But I'd like to suggest they often come into being in less dramatic and infinitely more satisfying ways.

What do I know of science on such a grand scale? Not much. But I do know the French writer Anaïs Nin said, "Each new friend represents a world in us, a world not born until they arrive. And it is only by this meeting that a new world is born."

Friday — **August 28**

THOMAS GUY started his working life selling poorly printed Bibles. Eventually he imported better copies from the Continent and obtained a charter from Oxford University to print even better copies. Then he made his fortune.

But along the way he supported alms-houses, built hospital wards, and founded Guy's Hospital. His will helped many homeless people and included funds to release prisoners from debtors' jails in three counties.

All of which makes me think that Thomas Guy didn't just sell the Bible – he read it, too.

SPLENDID ISOLATION

Saturday — **August 29**

IT was the title of the book that caught my attention. It was called "Beautiful Thoughts" by the missionary Henry Drummond. It was a compilation; a beautiful thought taken from one of his many books for each day of the year.

Oh, I know modern life is busy and demanding, but a beautiful thought a day shouldn't be too much to ask. Try it. You will make your life more beautiful in the process.

Sunday — **August 30**

JESUS knew it, and grandparents everywhere know it. What is it? Well, the Russian writer Fyodor Dostoevsky summed it up like this – "Love children especially for, like angels, they live to soften and purify our hearts and, as it were, to guide us."

In the love of our children and grandchildren, we might rediscover the purity we once had. In that way they bring us a little closer to heaven here on earth.

Monday — **August 31**

THE composer and pianist Franz Liszt arrived in a German town to give a recital. After he had been there a few hours a nervous woman came to his lodgings. She admitted that for several years she had been making her living as a piano teacher, claiming to have been a pupil of Liszt himself. She explained that she had been orphaned and had only her piano skills to live on. She had lied and she was sorry for it.

Liszt demanded that she play. Thinking he was seeking to find out how much she had defamed his reputation, the woman did her very best. Liszt coolly corrected her on a couple of points of technique, then told her she could now claim – honestly – to have been taught by him.

He could have been insulted, he might have sought reparation, or had the woman jailed. Instead he made the situation better. Franz Liszt was a great man in more ways than one.

September

Tuesday — **September 1**

AFTER the War of Independence, Britain and America had another brief "falling out" between 1812 and 1814. The crew of a large American ship boarded a Welsh coal boat in the Irish sea.

As the victors searched the smaller vessel, the American captain asked about a wooden box with a slit in the top. The Welsh captain explained the crew held a service every Sunday and took a collection in the box to support missionary workers.

The American, a religious man himself, ordered his crew back to their ship telling his counterpart, "It's no use me interfering with good folks like you."

How often would it be the case that if we knew more about our "enemy" we would find we're not so different after all?

Wednesday — **September 2**

A SUMMER'S day, blue skies, not a breath of wind, and the birds are singing happily. But we can all sing in the good times!

And then there's the Water Ouzel, a little bird, somewhat like a thrush, who prefers to live under noisy waterfalls and in rocky, fast-flowing streams. A "dipper", it finds its food beneath these foaming waters. No easy task, I am sure. But it sings all the year round!

So, here's to my new hero, the Water Ouzel, who shows that it is possible to sing when times are good – and keep singing even when the waters of life get a bit more tempestuous!

Thursday — **September 3**

I WONDER how many people Charlie Chaplin made laugh. A comic actor from the era before "talkies", his movies were shown all across the world and are still available today.

He once said, "A day without laughter is a day wasted." If we allocated a day to each person who laughed at his films I am sure they would add up to several lifetimes' worth of joy.

That laughter is important was Chaplin's guiding principle. Choose a guiding principle for yourself. Make it something wonderful. Then fill your life with un-wasted days!

Friday — **September 4**

THE photo in the exhibition was of a ballerina *en pointe*, or on her toes. But the photographer had focused on the shoes. No-one in the audience, watching the ballerina's lighter-than-air dancing, would have noticed that the blocks in the toes were worn and the silk around those parts of the shoes was tattered and frayed.

What was the point, or "*pointe*," the artist was making? Perhaps it was this; that we can all make our lives seem graceful and effortless – if, first of all, we put in the work!

Saturday — **September 5**

I DO think Harry may have discovered the secret of eternal youth – although you wouldn't think it as he holds his back after straightening up from doing the weeding!

"Of all the weeds that need pulling," he told me, "I hate uprooting dandelions most of all. I remember the fun I had with them, in all their stages, when I was but an innocent lad with no thought spared to the gardener's concerns."

The secret of eternal youth? It's nothing to do with dandelions, but it has a lot to do with staying in touch with the child you once were!

Sunday — **September 6**

I HEARD the church bells ringing,
And I heard the choir sing,
And, Lord, my heart was lifted up
For all the day could bring.
The promise of the week ahead,
No matter what it holds,
The knowledge, Lord, that you are close
As every day unfolds.
And so the music lifted me,
And carried me on high,
Now I'll go forward, Lord, with hope,
As every day goes by.
Iris Hesselden.

Monday — **September 7**

THE origin of the word gossip is the Middle English word "godsybbe" which means godparent!

It came to describe female friends gathered at a birth, and the kind of talk that would be shared, characterised by intimacy, candour, trust and hope for the future.

How I wish we could reclaim that meaning and indulge in a lot more of that kind of gossip!

Tuesday — **September 8**

IT'S pretty," my fellow visitor to the quaint seaside village said, "but boats were made for the sea." We were looking at a row-boat, pulled up to the roadside and filled with flowers.

I disagreed. The little dinghy would have had its time on the waves. Should it have stayed out there until it sank?

We will all have had a purpose, but when the time comes to pull up on to the beach of life, may we still have it in us to find a new, and possibly more beautiful, purpose!

Wednesday — **September 9**

THERE'S a wood where some creative soul has carved and painted signs apparently pointing the way to Narnia, the Shire, Hogwarts, Toad Hall, the Emerald City and Mr McGregor's Garden.

It's an enchanting thought that we might visit these places, but there is, however, one "magical" place that beats all of those as a destination. It's difficult to point out which direction it's in because that changes depending on who is looking.

It is, of course, Home!

Thursday — **September 10**

IF ever I have ventured near a washing machine with anything woollen the result has been disastrous. Wool requires careful handling, and yet sheep are out on the hills in all weather and their coats stay just as fluffy as ever!

The shepherds of old had an explanation, one we might apply to other frustrations in life. Sheep don't shrink in the rain, because they shake the water off.

So . . . shake it off, and don't shrink!

Friday — **September 11**

THERE may be a musical term for the dreadful groan when someone opens up an accordion or the asthmatic wheeze that usually begins any tune on the bagpipes.

Having said that, those noises will almost inevitably be followed by music that would make the stiffest of us feel like dancing.

So, don't worry about the awkwardness, or the embarrassment, that generally accompanies the beginning of a new venture. Get past the groan and the wheeze and let your music be heard!

Saturday — **September 12**

WOULD you like a cup of tea, a pot of tea – or a brick of tea? In days gone by, across China, Mongolia and Russia, tea would be ground and pressed into blocks, often with decorative patterns. These tea bricks could be traded, broken up and eaten – or could be made into tea! They were regularly used as currency.

We don't see tea bricks so often around here, but a relaxing cuppa or meeting friends for tea are still the blocks that many a satisfying day is built on!

Sunday — **September 13**

THERE must be an easier way to grow pretty flowers," I suggested.

Harry pushed his garden fork into the soil.

"I hear Thérèse of Lisieux used to imagine her good deeds as flowers. When she had enough for a bouquet she would send them to God, then he would spread them over the world in the form of blessings."

I thought about Thérèse as I walked on. A bouquet of good deed flowers might be a bit much for a beginner. But, if I keep my eyes open and my heart willing, I might be able to offer God a buttonhole or two.

Monday — **September 14**

HE has the patience of a rock," I said of a friend to Mary. "I'd rather have the patience of a flower," she said. "Waiting as a seed underground, preparing, putting out roots and shoots, growing into the sunshine, giving pleasure, helping feed the bees."

I knew I had been taught a lesson, even while I tried to figure out what it was. I suppose the true virtue of patience is not in how long you can wait, but in how you behave while you wait!

Tuesday — **September 15**

A BOOKSHOP had a collection of "Things We Found In Books" on their walls. There were theatre tickets, various bookmarks, a signed photo of a famous actor, a letter from a book club "on the occasion of the Coronation," and so on.

There's much more to be found inside books, like excitement, mystery, education, laughter. And if we find all that in ordinary books, how much more should we expect to find in the Bible? There's everything you'll find in other books, plus an explanation of the universe and our place in it. There's love, and there's life.

Wednesday — **September 16**

MARY'S niece, Lucy, was searching online for a music video. She typed in the words, *The Power Of* . . .

A drop-down menu offered dozens of options entitled "The Power of Love". But what surprised Lucy was how far she had to scroll before she found anything other than "love" in the list.

"Maybe nothing else is anywhere near as powerful," she suggested to her aunt.

"And there's no other power so well worth singing about," Mary added.

Thursday — **September 17**

HAVE you ever done a little kindness – something anyone might have done, something you didn't think was all that much – only to have the other person appreciate it beyond any expectation you might have had?

It's a wonderful feeling, isn't it?

A dear friend once summed that up by saying, "Never tire of doing little things for others. Sometimes those little things occupy the biggest part of their hearts!"

CONTINENTAL COLOUR!

Friday — **September 18**

THE 19th-century French writer Edmond de Goncourt must really have been missing his beloved when he wrote, "When we are parted, we each feel the lack of the other half of ourselves. That is what I imagine love to be: incompleteness in absence."

If I might suggest a slight alteration to Monsieur de Goncourt's thoughts, I would suggest that love isn't about incompleteness – it is about the desire to be complete; the need to be together.

Saturday — **September 19**

HOW many photos have you seen of people pretending to hold up the straight towers in Pisa? Not many. But thousands of people every year will visit the leaning tower.

The leaning tower is now a preserved monument and the Italian government spends a lot of money taking care of it, while other, straighter, towers will have fallen into disrepair.

The tower's architects didn't design it to lean, and our plans don't always turn out the way we want them to either. But, sometimes, they work out better!

Sunday — **September 20**

I WAS grumbling about being caught in the rain when George came along, looking as content in the wet as any duck. "The good Lord provides us with all we need," he said.

"Well, He didn't provide you with a hat in all this rain," I snapped.

"No," he replied. "But He did provide me with waterproof skin and that's all we need right now."

Because I wanted to get out of my wet clothes I hurried on. But I did feel a little bit of a drip about it so I promised to take a tip from George and give thanks for having my needs met – in shine and in rain!

Monday — **September 21**

A CALLER *came to see me; he didn't stay too long,*
He walked around my garden and told me what was wrong:
"Those buttercups and daisies – you've let them grow unchecked
And speedwell too, and poppies! My goodness – such neglect!"
I wondered – should I tell him I liked them flowering free,
And what he classed as "nuisance" brought naught but joy
to me?
But no, for all it shows you is – whether weed or rose –
There's beauty all around us, whichever place it grows!
Margaret Ingall.

Tuesday — **September 22**

W HISPERING galleries are circular balconies, usually under domes. The idea is that if you turn towards the wall and talk, or whisper, the sound of your voice will carry all around the gallery, so someone on the opposite side might hear it clearly.

Jean Paul Richter, the 17th century novelist, said, "The words we speak to our children in the privacy of the home are not heard by the world, but, as in whispering galleries, they are clearly heard at the end and by posterity."

So, like all our words, whispered or said out loud, we need to make them good ones.

Wednesday — **September 23**

T HERE are aspects of childhood even the most mature of us should hang on to. Talking about the joy children derive from every aspect of life, the essayist Charles Edward Montague wrote, "A child in the full health of his mind will put his hand flat on a summer lawn, feel it, and give a little shiver of private glee."

Do you remember moments like that? Good! Because Mr Montague also added that such delight "need not be lost, to the end of their day, by anyone who has ever had it."

Thursday — September 24

HAVE you ever found yourself swimming against the tide? Not literally, but in the sense of having to act against the general opinion. Judy found herself in that position when she left a well-paid job to work with young offenders.

"Despite the fact I myself felt sure I was doing the right thing, so many people expressed doubts that I began to question myself," she admitted. "Then I remembered the words of John Bunyan: 'I'll fear not what men say'." She smiled. "Just six words, but such powerful ones!"

Not surprising from a man whose strength of courage was legendary.

Friday — September 25

THERE'S a legend of a soldier being court-martialled by Alexander of Macedonia, then ruler of the known world. Believing his verdict to be unfair, the soldier wanted to appeal.

"Who can you appeal to," Alexander said, "who is above me?"

"Now I direct my appeal," the brave soldier replied, "from Alexander the Small to Alexander the Great!"

What would it be like if we would only live by our nobler ideals, be that higher version of ourselves in the ordinary days of our lives? I think it would be – you guessed it – great!

Saturday — September 26

IF you are a gardener, might I ask what you grow? Is your patch a delight of colour or an example of ordered necessity? Beautiful blooms? Humble veg? A combination of both? Might I suggest you cultivate more than that?

Mary Howitt, who wrote in England 150 years ago, put it this way: "Yes, in the poor man's garden grow far more than herbs and flowers – kind thoughts, contentments, peace of mind, and joy for weary hours."

A SIGHT
FOR SORE
EYES

Sunday — September 27

THE ship's compass was an impressive piece of work. The circular brass plate was beautifully engraved, showing all the major directions, with a starburst in the middle and an intricate pattern around. It was presented in a mahogany box and protected by a glass dome.

But the essence of the compass was the narrow, wavering, strip of magnetised steel – and the invisible force which, even in the highest seas, kept turning it back to the right direction.

Our lives might be impressive pieces of work, carefully crafted and beautifully presented. But all of that is superficial stuff.

What matters, in the calms and the storms of life, is whether the essence of us sits any old way, or turns in the right direction when the invisible force makes its presence felt.

Monday — September 28

IT doesn't seem to be for the best of reasons that around 1808 Sir William Hillary came to live on the Isle of Man.

Rumours of unpaid debts were said to be responsible for his departure from the mainland, but whatever the reason, the outcome was one to be blessed. For it was while living in this close proximity to the water that he came to realise just how dangerous the sea could be.

He published a pamphlet suggesting ways to help sea-farers in danger, and before long had persuaded several London philanthropists to offer practical help. Thus the organisation which we now know as the Royal National Lifeboat Institution came into being.

Nobody knows exactly how many lives have been saved over the years, but we can all thank God for those courageous volunteers who continue to put Sir William Hillary's inspiration into practice.

Tuesday — September 29

I'VE just been reading about a birthday party held by starlight on the shores of a lake in Exmoor. This, however, was no ordinary birthday party in honour of any one individual, for it was held to celebrate the anniversary of the setting up of a Dark Skies Discovery Site at Wimball Lake in Somerset.

In 2011, concerns about light pollution finally led to Exmoor National Park being designated the first International Dark Sky Reserve in Europe.

Within this area deliberate efforts have been made to ensure that artificial lighting is carefully managed, not only to benefit wildlife, but also to ensure that we humans may fully enjoy the wonder and magnificence of the night sky.

And if that's not worth switching off a light or two, I don't know what is!

Wednesday — September 30

THANK you, Lord, for bringing us
So safely through the night,
Through all the hours of darkness
Until the morning light.
Thank you, Lord, for being near
With love and healing touch
To take away the anxious thoughts
That trouble us so much.

Thank you for another day,
Whatever lies in store,
Please help us use it wisely
Till night-time comes once more.
Then help us feel your presence,
Your love and gentle care,
Reminding us both night and day
That you are always there.

Iris Hesselden.

October

Thursday — **October 1**

I COULD see the bunch of balloons bobbing down the street ahead of me, but it wasn't until I caught up with the person holding them that I realised it was Marion.

"I've been to my grandson's fifth birthday party." She grinned. "And he absolutely insisted that I take some balloons home with me. I couldn't refuse! And in fact I'm very glad I didn't. I don't think I've passed anyone yet who hasn't given me a smile or cheerful word."

What fun for Marion – but what a shame that it takes a bunch of balloons to break down our barriers. Let's try in future simply to imagine the balloons, and give each other a smile anyway!

Friday — **October 2**

SORRY

I 'M sorry" – they're such simple words,
Yet sometimes hard to say.
It's easier to turn one's head,
To shrug and walk away.
But if, deep down, we know we're wrong,
Then put it into speech!
Admitting that we've made mistakes
Can start to heal the breach.
Be bold and take that first brave step,
Don't let intentions drift,
For bridges that are built with love
Can span the widest rift!

Margaret Ingall.

Saturday — **October 3**

WHATEVER age we are, whatever our circumstances, every one of us can find ourselves facing a challenge which is tempting but rather scary! Which is why I really like this little quote.

"'It's impossible,' said pride.
'It's risky,' said experience.
'It's pointless,' said reason.
'Give it a try,' whispered the heart."

I don't know the author, but I salute his or her courage! May we all listen to our hearts, and may our lives be richer for it.

Sunday — **October 4**

I DON'T know if the American abolitionist and clergyman Henry Ward Beecher knew much about sailing, but he certainly knew about the Bible.

"The Bible," he said, "is God's chart for you to steer by, to keep you from the bottom of the sea, and to show you where the harbour is, and how to reach it without running on rocks."

In other words, an invaluable aid to guide us through the most troubled of waters.

Monday — **October 5**

SHEILA was scheduled for a week in hospital. Jane, her friend, had to be away so wouldn't be able to visit. Then she had an idea – a simple act of kindness.

Before her trip, Jane wrapped up seven small gifts, each with a little note, for Sheila to open each day she was in hospital. Jane knew they would make her smile.

And they did. When Sheila opened one of her little parcels she knew that her friend cared enough to make sure she was remembered every day. What could be nicer than that?

Tuesday — **October 6**

I CONFESS I did see the little penny on the pavement. The Lady of the House went one better.

She saw it and bent down to pick it up. She cleaned it with a tissue and dropped it in my jacket pocket.

I wondered why she bothered and it must have showed in my expression.

"A penny is like a hug," she said. "Not very important at all – until you really need one."

Wednesday — **October 7**

YES, I always wanted to, but . . ." It's amazing how easy it is for us to find excuses why we've never quite achieved an ambition. And equally amazing to see how often those who have succeeded have overcome countless obstacles in order to do so.

Which is why I like the Swedish proverb, "Those who wish to sing will always find a song".

May we all find our own song, and may we never let distractions stop us singing.

Thursday — **October 8**

HAVE you ever wished you could do something world-changing? I imagine that to most of us the mere idea seems so unlikely that we don't even consider how we might go about it.

Happily, Scottish singer Annie Lennox is not so easily deterred.

She says, "Ask yourself: 'Have you been kind today?' Make kindness your modus operandi, and change your world."

Not so impossible after all!

Friday — **October 9**

I'VE often heard it said that good health is worth more than money, but I've just come across a quotation which has made me realise that there's something even more important than that. It was American writer Og Mandino who said, "Treasure the love you receive above all. It will survive long after your gold and good health have vanished."

Saturday — **October 10**

THERE'S a tale I like from the days when Mount Everest seemed like an unconquerable peak. A mountaineer raised a toast at a gathering of like-minded souls.

"You defeated us once," he addressed the great mountain. "You defeated us twice. You defeated us three times. But, Everest, we shall some day defeat you because you can't get any bigger – and we can."

When your problems seem insurmountable, remember, they will always be what they are, but, like those brave mountaineers, you can always be bigger and better!

Sunday — **October 11**

GEORGE was a farmer before illness forced him to turn the running of the farm over to his son. He admits he thought he had lost all purpose. But – discovering the leisure time which farmers never have – George got involved in disability groups, travelled to churches far and wide talking about faith, and found a new lease of life in his grandchildren.

Visiting, I commented that I had never seen him so bright, which made a change from the pouring rain I had braved to get there.

"Well, God sends the sunshine and the rain," George said, "and he sends them both to be a blessing!"

If anyone knew the truth of that, it would be George.

Monday — **October 12**

KATY is a primary school teacher and, as much as she loves her job and her pupils, admits that it is challenging.

"But today," she told me, "as I was teaching the children about China, I came across something that made me stop and think. We were talking about silk worms when I found the following Chinese proverb: 'With time and patience, the mulberry leaf becomes a silk gown'." She grinned.

"A lesson there for me, too, I think!"

Tuesday — **October 13**

IF at first you don't succeed – just hide all the evidence that you tried." I must admit that when I read that joke I had to chuckle, for it does sum up the way we all hate to admit that we've been defeated.

However, on second, more serious thoughts, I think such sentiments rather a pity. After all, I very much doubt if anyone in the world can succeed at everything they ever attempt – but the real shame would be not even to try.

It takes courage to dare to undertake something we've never done before, so even if you never do quite succeed – be proud – at least you tried!

Wednesday — **October 14**

FEAR not, the Lord is with us!
Let no-one be dismayed,
His love will hold us safely,
His strength will be our aid.
That promise of God's caring
Is in the Bible vowed,
So let our thanks be joyful,
Our praise for him sung loud.

Margaret Ingall.

PERTHSHIRE'S AUTUMN SHOW

Thursday — **October 15**

HERE'S a word for you to add to your vocabulary," Bill said. "It's 'googolplex', and it means the highest number you can think of – and then keep adding some more!"

"It's a great word," I agreed, "but I have to say that I'm not sure I'd have a great deal of use for it."

"No?" Bill asked with a smile. "Ever tried counting your blessings?"

Ah, yes – perhaps it's a word I shall be needing, after all!

Friday — **October 16**

OF all things, it was a study on how well the human body is adapted to walking that reminded me of a saying of my grandmother's.

"While one foot walks, the other rests," the study's author had written, unknowingly quoting Grannie. He meant it to reflect the efficiency of the body. She meant it as a description of family, or of friends, who helped each other.

So, as we walk through this life let us follow the example of our feet; let us rest while someone bears the load, and bear the load while someone rests!

Saturday — **October 17**

HAVE you ever noticed, Francis," Fred mused as we fell to putting the world to rights, "that it's usually those people who have the most to lose who are most willing to take chances?"

I suspect he's right. It was in a radio interview that I once heard that great actor Jack Lemmon being asked if he feared failure. "No," he replied, "for once you give in to that, then it stops you from ever trying anything new."

I think there is inspiration in those words for all of us. Life is too precious not to live it to its fullest.

Sunday — October 18

THE film director David Lean had talked about his dream of a fourth step on the podium at sporting events for the one who had made the greatest improvement! It reminded my friend Mary of an expression her father used. When someone had tried but fallen short he would say, "He did his poor best."

Most of our bests are poor efforts next to experts with more resources or more natural ability, but it is always worth trying. Imagine how different awards ceremonies (and life) would be if we rewarded not the fastest or strongest, but the one who tried the hardest.

Those "poor" bests would probably be wonderful indeed!

Monday — October 19

THERE is no doubt that we live in a world of wonders. Almost every day we can open our newspapers to read of a new invention or discovery. We can switch on a television or a computer (wonders in themselves!) and learn of all sorts of amazing things.

We are so accustomed to marvels, in fact, that we can take such things for granted. Ralph Waldo Emerson reminds us that something doesn't have to be new in order to be entirely awe inspiring: "The creation of a thousand forests is in one acorn".

And that's just one of the everyday miracles around us!

Tuesday — October 20

ONCE mankind had the best garden of all and then we were turned out. Gardens are harder to find in today's built-up and busy world. But still an army of good souls tend the earth, some traditionally and others in more imaginative ways.

To all the green-fingered souls I dedicate this thought from Amos Bronson Alcott, an early 19th century teacher: "Who loves a garden still his Eden keeps. Perennial pleasures, plants and wholesome harvest reaps."

Wednesday — October 21

SUPPOSE I said you really ought to be happy – for other people's sake! But, you see, if you're happy you are likely to be kinder, your joy will lighten other people's days. Then their happiness will lift you in turn!

Robert Louis Stevenson said, "There is no duty we so much underrate as the duty of being happy. Being happy, we sow anonymous benefits upon the world."

Then the world does the same to us!

Thursday — October 22

DO you watch the "Time Team" on television? If so, you'll know just how important a geophysical survey can be on an archaeological dig. For even when little or nothing is visible to the naked eye, a geophysical examination can show just where long-gone buildings or earth works once existed.

There's something rather inspiring about that. It's easy sometimes, when we try to make the world a better place, to feel that our efforts have disappeared without trace.

And yet even when they do seem forgotten or ineffective, I'm quite sure our actions do leave their mark. We just haven't yet invented a machine to measure them!

Friday — October 23

A SOCIETY gentleman once announced that there were only about 400 people in New York worth knowing. The writer O. Henry reproved him by entitling his next collection of stories "The Four Million". To him everyone was worth knowing and he was sure they all had stories to tell.

We simply have to expand O. Henry's idea, moving beyond the limits of the city, to see know how God sees us. He knows we have stories worth telling, because He wrote them!

Saturday — **October 24**

I KNEW Malvina Reynolds was a singer songwriter,"Jenny said, "and I love her songs like 'Little Boxes' and 'Morningtown Ride'. But I didn't know she also had a good line in riddles. Try this, Francis: what is it that the more you give away, the more you end up with?"

Before I had a chance to think, Jenny was grinning. "Love!"

That's a great riddle. And the songs aren't bad either!

Sunday — **October 25**

HAVE you ever built an altar? They can be humble set-ups, quiet places of prayer, or they can be fabulously ornate arrangements of the kind we see in churches or cathedrals.

No doubt the French novelist Victor Hugo had seen many of both kinds before he expressed his preference. "The most beautiful of altars," he wrote, "is the soul of an unhappy creature, consoled and thanking God."

And each of us can lend a hand in building one of those.

Monday — **October 26**

I HAD an aunt," Jeannie told me, "who was a philosopher in her own way. She didn't have much money, so if she mentioned a treat that was beyond her means, she would always add, 'But I'm sure I wouldn't have liked it anyway'."

Jeannie chuckled at the memory.

"I soon realised she wasn't being serious, but I also came to understand that there was a lot to recommend that attitude.

"My aunt certainly had her dreams, but never made herself unhappy by hankering after the unobtainable. It taught me that contentment can be found just as easily in the small things, as in expensive outward trappings."

As Buddha reminds us, "Contentment is the greatest wealth".

Tuesday — **October 27**

WE all love opening parcels, but Yorkshire writer H.L. Gee had an unusual take on it. Back in the Thirties, Gee often set off on walking tours, then wrote about people he met.

Speaking to a man he met on his travels, he said, "Are you not one of the millions of universes we call men and women, all bundles of surprises, and every one worth unpacking?"

Why not try "unpacking" a friend, a neighbour, or someone you've just met. Like Mr Gee, you may be pleasantly surprised.

Wednesday — **October 28**

HOW would you define the word "home"? During a meal with friends, the one classification on which we all agreed was that it should be a place where we can happily and unapologetically be ourselves.

Afterwards, on the way home, the Lady of the House and I continued to ponder on the matter. For if this good Earth is home to its whole population, wouldn't it be wonderful if we could indeed all live without fear or pretence?

It's Max Ehrmann's poem "Desiderata" that contains the line "You are a child of the universe . . . you have a right to be here".

We may not be able to do much about the rest of the world, but in our own little part of it, let's try to ensure it's always a welcoming and accepting place to be.

Thursday — **October 29**

IT was supposed to be a description of confidence but it meant a little more to me.

"Confidence," the unknown philosopher stated, "is realising that although you aren't the best at something, you still enjoy doing it."

I smiled. You see, knowing I'm not the best but still enjoying it anyway is how I live my life!

And I hope you are just as confident!

Friday — **October 30**

WHEN Jenny was a teenager, she wasn't at all pleased when her father's change of job meant uprooting the family to the far side of the country. She was upset at the thought of leaving all her friends and everything that was familiar to her.

"It took me some time to learn that it was in my own best interest to think positive," she admitted. "But it's a lesson that has stood me in good stead through the rest of my life.

"In fact, I once read some words of Robert Fulghum, which put it really well:

'The grass is not, in fact, always greener on the other side of the fence. No, not at all. Fences have nothing to do with it. The grass is greenest where it is watered. When crossing over fences, carry water with you and tend the grass where ever you may be'."

If you should find yourself having to move, do make sure you pack that watering-can!

Saturday — **October 31**

IT'S so you!" our young friend announced, addressing the Lady of the House. "What a good choice."

We all laughed as the item in question was a new umbrella on its first outing in the rain. The design had small white butterflies and, around the edge, small pink and black cats.

We continued on our way in the rain, but more and more I became aware of other umbrellas bobbing along around us.

One in particular had all the colours of the rainbow, and another, a border of spring flowers. A little girl, trotting along beside her mother and trying to look very grown up, had her own umbrella. This had a smiling face on the front and two large ears on the top. It gave everyone a smile and the Lady of the House remarked, "That's a jolly brolly!"

We returned home feeling much more cheerful. Isn't it surprising how much colour we can still find on a grey day and how uplifting that can be.

November

Sunday — **November 1**

SAY the word "courage", and I suppose most people's first thoughts are of dramatic deeds of derring-do.

But sometimes courage can take a more passive, yet just as demanding, form – such as simply hanging on to our faith in times of trouble, and trusting that all will be well.

It's then that we can gain most comfort from Our Lord's promise: "So I say to you, Ask and it will be given to you, seek and you will find; knock and the door will be opened to you."

Powerful words for times when we are most in need.

Monday — **November 2**

IF you know the action stories of writer Andy McNab, you'll probably also be aware that he has a wealth of experience to draw from, including overcoming a difficult upbringing and achieving a most impressive career as a soldier.

So when asked what piece of wisdom he'd pass on to a child, I wasn't surprised that his answer was "No matter what you're doing, give it your absolute best."

But even more pleasing to me was his added advice: "And never forget to stop and appreciate what you have achieved."

I'd say that latter point is particularly important, whatever age we are.

Accomplishments don't have to be spectacular in order to be important – and sometimes we're so busy dwelling on the things we haven't done that we forget to be pleased about what we have achieved.

If you've given it your best, be proud!

RUSHING BY

Tuesday — **November 3**

ALEC WAUGH was strolling through St James's Park one November evening. The lights and the mist must have combined perfectly to stop him, captivated, on the bridge over the lake. The city, just for a moment, seemed like something out of "The Arabian Nights".

On his travels he saw beautiful sights but he often thought he might have seen as many had he stayed at home and had more "moments of surprised delight" like that one.

Might we, too, see familiar places in new, wondrous ways if we looked with eyes prepared to be surprised and delighted?

Wednesday — **November 4**

NOBODY'S perfect," the old saying tells us. But what if we could be more perfect?

Well . . . if we want to be fitter we exercise, if we want to be smarter we study, but coming closer to perfection . . .

I'd be stuck if I hadn't read these words from the 17th century Dutch philosopher Benedict de Spinoza, who said, "The more joy we have, the more nearly perfect we are."

That sounds like the perfect self-improvement regime!

Thursday — **November 5**

THE poet and novelist Anatole France spoke of a majestic old oak at Fontainebleau; he mentioned a priceless painting in the Louvre and books of philosophy in a library. To the list he added fresh air, rivers, forests and sunlight.

He declared that no wealthy man owned them more than he did. In fact, he could be said to own them more than the wealthy man because he appreciated them more!

Why not add to your wealth by including the things money can't buy? Then become richer still through appreciation!

Friday — **November 6**

OH, for those beautiful summery days when the days are so long we might forget to close our curtains from one day to the next! Are they just a memory, or a distant hope, in the depths of winter?

Not necessarily. Why not visit friends, or invite them round and have fun together? After all, as William Makepeace Thackeray, the 19th century novelist, once said, "A good laugh is sunshine in a house."

Saturday — **November 7**

WHAT would you do if you came into money? I always find it encouraging that so many people's first thoughts are not of the treats they would buy themselves, but of the gifts they would give.

It was French philosopher Denis Diderot who said, "Happiest are the people who give most happiness to others".

But do remember – we don't actually have to wait for that windfall to make a difference. Sometimes something as simple as a smile can transform someone's day!

Sunday — **November 8**

WHEN Tom and Sarah moved into their new house they knew that they would need alterations done which would involve several days of noisy building work.

"So, as a kind of forward apology to our neighbours, we decided to invite them to a teaparty," Sarah said. "Just as we hoped, once we explained what would be happening, they were all very understanding.

"But even better," she continued, smiling, "it turned out that very few of them really knew each other, so our tea party turned into a proper getting-to-know-you event!"

Sounds as if a few friendships may have been built, as well as that new extension!

Monday — **November 9**

IT'S as true for the difficult times in life as it is for the long, wet and windy months. Hal Borland, who wrote "outdoor editorials" for the New York Times, wrote, "No winter lasts for ever, no spring skips its turn."

Persevere just a little longer with difficulties and short, dull days. The flowers of spring are just around the corner.

Tuesday — **November 10**

DO you know anyone who only ever speaks wisely and who never comes out with anything rather foolish? No, I don't either, and that includes myself!

Which is why I particularly like to remind you of the words of George Eliot, who wrote: "A friend is one to whom one may pour out the contents of one's heart, chaff and grain together, knowing that gentle hands will take and sift it, keep what is worth keeping, and with a breath of kindness, blow the rest away."

May we all have friends like that. And may we all be friends like that!

Wednesday — **November 11**

WINSTON CHURCHILL'S life might easily be seen as one of achievement and success. He came back from a political wilderness to lead Britain through World War II, he won a Nobel Prize for his writing and he was the first person ever to be made an honorary citizen of the United States.

It might have been difficult for some to pick a crowning glory from a life like that, but Churchill had his priorities right.

"My most brilliant achievement," he once said, "was my ability to be able to persuade my wife to marry me."

Loving and being loved are surely the greatest achievements in anybody's life – and Churchill knew it!

Thursday — **November 12**

LIFE is full of difficult choices. John Steinbeck would have known that as well as any of us, but he also knew that, in the end, there was only one question that mattered.

"A man," he wrote, "after he has brushed off the dust and chips of his life, will have left only the hard, clean question: was it good or was it evil? Have I done well or ill?"

Keeping that question in mind will, I am sure, make those difficult decisions a whole lot simpler.

Friday — **November 13**

BEN, who recently moved up into "big" school, had been struggling to get to grips with the subject of geometry. However, when I saw him on his way home after class, he was looking much more cheerful.

"I'm getting a bit better at last." He grinned. "My teacher gave me some good advice. He told me that the best angle from which to approach any problem is the 'try-angle'."

Guaranteed to save anyone going round in circles!

Saturday — **November 14**

I ABSOLUTELY knew it would be the right job for me," Angela said. "And I prayed nightly that I'd be offered the position." She laughed. "That was twenty years ago, and I can't tell you how glad I am that it didn't happen. If it had, then I'd never have been spurred into exploring other avenues, never run my own business, or even met my husband. Thank goodness that God knew better than I did."

Her experience reminded me of some lyrics from the Garth Brooks song: "Some of God's greatest gifts are unanswered prayers". Not the sort of gift we may relish at the time, but oh, how valuable they prove to be!

Sunday — November 15

*FOR surely Thy goodness and mercy
Will follow me all of my days."
What comfort that promise can bring us,
What cause for rejoicing and praise!
May always those words reassure us
We're never too lost from God's sight,
He always will find us and lead us
Once more to the pathways of light.*

Margaret Ingall.

Monday — November 16

I MUST admit," Barbara said, "these days I always try to treat my worries in the same way I treat spiders."

Seeing my surprise, she explained.

"I know it's silly, but I've never been very keen on them, and if I ever saw one indoors it really bothered me. Then I slowly came to realise that even if I did glimpse a spider, it would always scuttle away and I'd never see it again. So I made a conscious decision not to think about them – and if the worst happened, and a spider didn't disappear of its own accord, well then, I'd ask a friend to help me."

I rather like that philosophy. So often the things that worry us never actually materialise. And if they do, the presence of friends can be a wonderful aid to frightening them away!

Tuesday — November 17

IN Jules Verne's "Around The World In Eighty Days" Phileas Fogg risks delaying his journey, and losing his fortune, to rescue an Indian princess. They are married shortly afterwards.

When we think of the benefits that come from kindness, both for the recipients and the instigators, it really is amazing that people ever waste time doing anything else – anywhere around the world!

Wednesday — **November 18**

THE harp has to be one of the most beautiful instruments to listen to. But have you ever watched a harpist? It's not all about plucking the strings. It's also about laying hands on the strings to stop their vibrations; to bring the notes to an end.

In a world that seems to be all about getting things done we might learn a thing or two from the harpist. There's a time to vibrate and a time to be still. It's the skilful balance of those two opposites that can make any life seem like a beautiful melody.

Thursday — **November 19**

SHIRLEY TEMPLE played Mytyl in the 1940s movie "The Bluebird Of Happiness". The spoiled little Swiss girl travels with her little brother and a fairy godmother through the past, the present and the future in search of the fabled bird.

She doesn't find it! But she becomes a better person through the search – and finds the bluebird waiting for her when she returns home.

The journey to happiness can often be a difficult one, but the bird is always there within us waiting for us to let it fly free. And that's nothing to be blue about.

Friday — **November 20**

THESE days there are kinds of treatments that claim to keep your skin wrinkle free – but what if you want to go a bit deeper? Educator and philosopher Amos Bronson Alcott recommended this cost-free regime a century and a half ago:

"To keep the heart unwrinkled be hopeful, kindly, cheerful and reverent."

Lots of therapies have side-effects, of course, and this is no exception. Fortunately, the side-effects of Mr Alcott's prescription all involve having a happier life!

Saturday — **November 21**

SOMETHING tells me the comic actress Gilda Radner was a dog person. The clue was when she said, "I think dogs are the most amazing creatures; they give unconditional love. For me, they are the role model for being alive."

I've known dogs like that, and cats, ponies, parakeets, and all sorts of animals. But there's a special place in my heart for the people I know who try to live like that.

As far as examples of how to live a good life go, Ms Radner's surely has to take the biscuit!

Sunday — **November 22**

I HAVE often heard Frank refer to his "wee days out", usually in Glasgow, Edinburgh or Stirling. A busy man, he usually manages to go once or twice a month, but it was only recently I asked him what he did.

"Oh, that's when I attend to my divine appointments," he told me with a shy smile.

In other words, he looks out for the people God puts in his way and talks with them, helps them, or learns from them.

"I've been doing it for years," he explained. "Sometimes there are no appointments, but mostly there are, and those are the best 'business meetings' I ever have!"

Monday — **November 23**

AMY wasn't sure if she should stay at her convenient, undemanding job or take the offer of a new, exciting, but uncertain, position.

"It's times like this that I wish we could live life backwards. Then there would never be any difficult decisions."

Sometimes we just have to take that leap of faith which – even if it doesn't work out as ideally as we'd hoped – can still enrich us in other ways.

STILL WATERS . . .

Tuesday — **November 24**

THE Lady of the House was smiling when she returned from visiting our good friend Maureen.

"We've been talking about talents," she told me, "and Maureen was bemoaning the fact that she didn't feel she was much good at anything in particular.

"I had to point out to her that she actually had the most wonderful natural gift for friendship. She's a superb listener, she's always willing to help, she empathises with other people's sorrows, and rejoices in their celebrations."

Quite an impressive list – and perhaps the most appreciated talent that anyone can cultivate!

Wednesday — **November 25**

THIS is the day the Lord hath made,
Rejoice!" the Bible says,
"This is the day the Lord hath made;
Be glad, and give Him praise."
For what a wondrous gift is this,
This precious shining day,
A chance to live, to love, to laugh,
Beginning right away!

Margaret Ingall.

Thursday — **November 26**

ST ANDREW'S Day, Christmas, Hogmanay, Up Helly Aa; someone once pointed out that the Scots seem to have most of their celebrations in the darkest part of the year.

But then, when are any of us in greater need of a celebration?

So if you find yourself or a friend going through a "dark" time, shine some light in it by finding something to celebrate!

Friday — **November 27**

ADOPT the pace of nature – her secret is patience." That advice came from Ralph Waldo Emerson, the American philosopher whose work and writings of a hundred years ago are still much respected.

But – adopt the pace of nature? Oh, surely not – that's much too slow! Or so I thought the first time I read that quotation.

Then I looked through the window. Beyond the mature copper-beech hedge I myself had planted, a glorious old oak tree reached strong and sturdy towards the sky.

And even farther away, I could see the hills whose familiar loveliness had been carved over numberless centuries.

Would they have looked any more magnificent for being a rush job? On reflection – I think not.

Perhaps Emerson got it right after all!

Saturday — **November 28**

I HAVE walked that stretch of coastline innumerable times. Sometimes I stop a while and watch the waves, sometimes I hurry on by, and sometimes I just want to stand there for ever and let the beauty of it all sweep me away.

What is it that makes such a big difference to what I see from one visit to the next? What is it that turns breaking waves into a crystal explosion; turns a still sea into a pool of contemplation; turns the simple sand into a wonder you just need to explore with your fingertips?

It's the quality of the light! And as I realised this I also understood that we, too, can be light in other people's lives.

Let's make sure our light is of the very best quality.

For you were once darkness, but now you are light in the Lord. Live as children of light. Ephesians 5:8.

Sunday — **November 29**

"THERE is no good news these days." I sighed as I glanced at my newspaper at the breakfast table.

"Well," the Lady of the House said, "the sun rose this morning and it was a glorious dawn. A blackbird sang outside the window and lots of others joined in. The grass sparkled with dewdrops and the shrubs look beautiful after last night's rain. There's plenty of good news if you look for it, Francis!"

How right she was. It was not the kind of news that gets into the papers, but it put a spring in my step for the rest of the day.

Monday — **November 30**

THANK you, Lord, for colours,
All the beauty we can share,
The wonder of the earth and sky
Around us everywhere.
The colours of a rainbow
Reaching out across the land,
The deep blue of the ocean
Caressing golden sand.
Thank you, Lord, for autumn rain
Though leaves come tumbling down,
There's red and yellow, green and gold,
And shades of rust and brown.
And through the grey of winter
As sunrise lights the sky,
It warms our hearts with hope and joy
As winter passes by.
And so, through spring and summer,
Through cloudy days or bright,
We thank you, Lord, for colours
And our precious gift of sight.

Iris Hesselden.

December

WE happened to be giving a lift to a young French exchange student when the Lady of the House suddenly noticed that his expression had changed to one of horror.

Cat's Eyes Removed, the road sign said – and it took some explaining on our part to reassure him that it meant nothing more sinister than a warning to drivers to take extra care.

Although the incident ended in laughter, it did make me realise just how easy it can be to leap to the most worrying conclusion.

So next time I see or hear something that tempts me to think the worst, I shall try to remember those cat's eyes, and remind myself that not everything is as alarming as it might first seem!

Wednesday — **December 2**

THERE are many stories which have been handed down to us from the North American Indians and this is one of my favourites:

Once there was a great forest fire, and all the birds and animals rushed to escape. Hummingbird went to the river and collected a drop of water.

The other birds laughed. "What are you doing?" they asked.

She replied, "I'm doing what I can."

Perhaps that should be our aim in life – simply to do what we can. We may not be able to make a great deal of difference in this large and troubled world, but, like the hummingbird, let us all do what we can, and I'm sure the collective effort will be worthwhile – and the results rewarding.

Thursday — **December 3**

'M so grateful for it!" our old friend Mary said. I quickly tried to recall if we'd sent her a card or a gift . . .

"It makes all the difference!" she insisted. "It costs nothing but it's absolutely priceless. It can turn the day around, make a bad situation good, lighten a heavy heart and can be applied with no training or notice whatsoever!"

I blush to think how clueless I undoubtedly looked.

"I'm grateful for gratitude, Francis!"

Gratitude! All too often we think of it as the thing that comes along after a gift. But, as our dear friend reminded me, it is surely a wonderful gift in its own right, and one we ought constantly to be grateful for!

Friday — **December 4**

HAVE you ever heard of Agnes Weston? Born in 1840, she was the daughter of a barrister, and her work might have begun and ended with the writing of a few temperance tracts, had she not chosen to turn theory into action by opening a coffee bar for troops.

As the often homesick young men were posted abroad she started writing to many of them, a kindly act which was so appreciated that she was soon sending a newsletter to thousands of sailors.

By now firmly committed to their care, she was instrumental in opening the first "Sailors' Rest" – a house outside the Devonport dockyard which provided food and beds, and which quickly led to the opening of other similar establishments.

Official recognition of her efforts eventually resulted in her being created a Dame, yet I suspect she relished even more the affectionate title of "Mother" Weston, bestowed upon her by all those she had helped.

She died in 1918 and was buried with full Naval honours – a tribute she undoubtedly deserved.

Saturday — **December 5**

THE sign in the shop window read, *We buy junk. We sell precious artefacts.*

The items going in would be the same as the items going out. The difference was how the shop owner looked at them.

So how are you going to look at your day today? Is it going to be disposable – bric-à-brac? Or will you see the potential, apply some TLC, and turn your day into a precious artefact?

Sunday — **December 6**

MANDY was delighted to have her Christmas shopping all done. And she was especially pleased with one gift. Ever since she was a child, when she asked her dad what he wanted for Christmas he would reply, "Peace on earth."

Usually she dismissed it and bought him a book, or socks.

"But this year," she told me, "I've made a start on getting him what he wanted." She had bought him a card and written the story inside of how she had made up with someone she hadn't talked to for years.

Peace on earth starts with little moments like that.

Monday — **December 7**

SAM was sixteen and busy in his bedroom revising for school exams. After two long hours he heard a gentle knock at the door. It was his dad with coffee and biscuits.

"How's it going, son? All this revision shows you're trying your best no matter what."

Sam grinned at his father. "Thanks, Dad," he said. "Hey – did you know these biscuits are my favourites? Awesome!"

"As your kids grow, they may forget what you said, but they won't forget how you made them feel." Kevin Heath (the founder of More4kids and Parenting Expert).

WINTER'S TOUCH

Tuesday — December 8

MANY things to many people,
Gifts and parties, candle glow,
Hymns for carols, prayers for healing,
Holly berries, mistletoe.
Times of sadness, lonely feelings,
Memories to fill the nights,
Children's faces, bright eyes shining,
Santa's grotto, fairy lights.

Stories of the Christmas angel,
One enduring, guiding star,
Shepherds in the fields abiding,
Wise men travelling afar.
Christmas has another meaning,
Here and now or far away,
Hope and peace and love for sharing,
Make it Christmas every day!

Iris Hesselden.

Wednesday — December 9

IF you were an international celebrity, I suspect it might be easy to forget that there's a world outside your own situation.

Entertainer Eddie Cantor, born in 1892, was an early and hugely popular star in the infant spheres of cinema and radio, but instead of just sitting back and enjoying his fame and fortune, he used his renown for good and, amongst other things, raised large sums of money to combat polio.

He is quoted as saying, "Slow down and enjoy life. It's not only the scenery you miss by going too fast – you also miss the sense of where you are going and why."

I think that's brilliant advice for all of us on life's journey – even if we don't happen to be a film star!

Thursday — **December 10**

WHEN I met Geoff on his way home from town, he was heavily laden.

"There was a sale at the garden centre," he said, as I commiserated with him over the large unwieldy bundles he carried. "And don't forget, there's something even heavier to carry – and that's a grudge!"

How true – and I shall try to remember that the next time I'm overburdened!

Friday — **December 11**

WALKING through the park next to the Houses of Parliament I noticed the Buxton Fountain. It was built in the 19th century by Charles Buxton – and I think I would have liked the man.

Running a business, giving to good causes, and being an MP, he probably had more duties than most. He may have failed in some, or carried out them all out in good style.

Regardless, it was his philosophy I liked. "You have not fulfilled every duty," he wrote, "Unless you have fulfilled that of being pleasant."

Saturday — **December 12**

I READ of an old cowboy walking into a hotel elevator. He glanced at the others there, said, "Good evening, men," then turned to face the doors.

But every other man in the elevator straightened and stood a little taller. They were reacting to his expectation of them and because he presented a "manly" example.

We wouldn't have to be cowboys to have a similar influence on those around us. We could call each other "friend" – and set the example by really being one.

Sunday — **December 13**

EVERY now and again I will walk in the garden of an evening and look up at the moon. Decades after it happened it is still an awesome thought that men journeyed there and actually walked on its dusty surface.

It's hard to imagine what could possibly compare with such an event, but James Irwin, who visited our nearest neighbour on Apollo 15, had his own thoughts about that.

"God walking on the earth," he once said, "is infinitely greater than man walking on the moon."

Monday — **December 14**

WHEN he was aged fifty-seven, Francis Charles Chichester was told that he had quite a serious illness.

But instead of thinking that his life was over, he decided instead that this was the perfect time to begin an adventure. In 1966, he set out in his yacht, *Gipsy Moth IV,* and became the first person to sail single-handed around the globe.

On his return to Plymouth nine months later, thousands of people gathered to welcome him home. He was such an inspiration that, in the following year, he was knighted.

No matter what obstacles we find along life's path, if we can find courage and determination, those obstacles can be overcome.

Tuesday — **December 15**

WE'VE all heard the saying "Look after the pennies and the pounds will take care of themselves." The children's writer Maria Edgeworth had a less financial and more beautiful take on the idea when she wrote, "If we take care of the moments then the years will take care of themselves."

And if we had years made up of well-tended moments then we probably wouldn't care what the pennies and pounds were up to!

Wednesday — **December 16**

WE all appreciate the people who keep public gardens looking good. No less will we appreciate the householders who keep their front gardens as a delight for passers-by. But how often do we give thanks to those gardeners who might never run their fingers through the soil, for theirs is a different kind of cultivation?

The novelist Marcel Proust had them in mind when he urged us to "Be grateful to the people who make us happy; they are the charming gardeners who make our souls blossom."

Thursday — **December 17**

DO you know, I quite surprised myself," Paul said. He was telling me of how he'd become involved with the after-school science club, having been "volunteered" by his grandson. Paul had been very unsure of his abilities either to keep order, or to impart knowledge in an interesting way, but happily was soon proved wrong. Now membership is thriving, with the children's activities encompassing everything from microscopes to telescopes!

As another scientist, Thomas Edison once observed: "If we did things we are capable of, we would astound ourselves."

Friday — **December 18**

I KNOW Eddie enjoys gardening but I was surprised when he hailed me from someone else's garden.

"We were grumbling about today's lack of neighbourliness," he explained. "And I suddenly thought that instead of complaining, I could be doing something about it!"

Eddie's story reminded me of Leo Tolstoy's saying: "Everyone thinks of changing the world, but no-one thinks of changing himself."

And that surely is the most effective place to start.

SANCTUARY WITHIN

Saturday — **December 19**

GARDENS! Much as I love them they take a lot of work. But the poet Henry Wadsworth Longfellow talks of a new kind of garden; one you can take with you; one that requires no spades, rakes and secateurs; one that might blossom in all four seasons. It's enough to make gardeners of us all!

"Kind hearts are the gardens
Kind thoughts are the roots
Kind words are the flowers
Kind deeds are the fruits
Take care of your garden
And keep out the weeds
Fill it with sunshine
Kind words and kind deeds."

Sunday — **December 20**

I WAS recently given a book of children's prayers and letters to God. They are all delightful, amusing and often quite touching. I would like to share some of them with you and I'm sure you will understand why I found them so appealing.

This first one made me realise how, as adults, we don't always appreciate the beauty around us:

"Dear God, You made a beautiful world for us to live in. We'd like to thank you for the world. Best wishes, Simon."

And another thank you letter:

"Dear God, I like nice people, cartoons, books, the sun and flowers. I don't like bad people, dirt, guns, things that hurt me. Thank you very much, Leo."

This obviously from a small child feeling quite grown up:

"Dear God, I can answer the telephone by myself now, so if You want to call I can say 'hello'. From Jake."

How simple things are to children. Why do we grown-ups make life so complicated? God bless them all!

Monday — **December 21**

THE Lady of the House is a member of a friendship group who meet on a regular basis. A curious new neighbour asked what happened on these occasions and there was a pause before she received a reply.

With a smile, the Lady of the House explained how each week was different, depending on the activities of each person, and their circumstances.

"We discuss many topics. Read uplifting poems or prose. Sometimes," she continued, "we just sit quietly and let the peace recharge our batteries. We share togetherness."

"I like the sound of that," our neighbour answered. "Please may I join?"

The reply was, "Yes, of course, you will be welcome."

Aren't we all in need of a little quietness, but also a bit of togetherness?

Tuesday — **December 22**

COLIN had been enjoying a weekend visit from his two small grandsons.

"They're grand little lads," he confided, "but a bit too young to understand about sharing peaceably. Still, I suppose it's all a bit like learning to play a musical instrument."

My bemusement must have shown in my face.

"When you first start learning an instrument, it seems really hard," he explained, "but the more you do it, the more enjoyable it is. Exactly like the art of sharing."

It isn't a way I'd ever looked at it before, but I do rather like it. Just as we get joy from making music, so we get joy from sharing.

For, as Seneca observed a very long time ago, "There is no delight in owning anything unshared."

Wednesday — **December 23**

NEWSPAPERS can often be so full of bad news that I was surprised to see Greg look up from his with a grin.

"I've just been reading about a man who retired and sold up his multi-million business – and gave away all the proceeds to good causes." He pointed to the page. "And if you look at his photo, he's wearing the biggest smile you'll ever see!"

What an uplifting story. I think it was the American journalist George Horace Lorimer who observed that "It's good to have money and the things that money can buy, but it's good, too, to check up once in a while and make sure that you haven't lost the things that money can't buy."

I suspect that businessman has found much more than he gave away.

Thursday — **December 24**

YOU know, Francis," the Lady of the House observed thoughtfully, "sometimes it can take a lot of strength to admit weakness.

"I'm thinking of Gwen," she continued. "She's always so generous with her time and efforts, always first to volunteer. But after that bad bout of flu she had, she was turning down all offers of assistance, even though she could have done with it.

"But I bumped into one of her neighbours this afternoon, who was all smiles because at last Gwen has agreed to accept some help with shopping and cooking."

Good for Gwen. Even though everyone likes to be the strong one, just occasionally it can be more generous to allow others to take on that role.

I agree with the words of George Eliot, who said, "What do we live for, if it is not to make life less difficult for each other?"

Friday — December 25

WAITING, watching, wondering,
Counting every day,
Wishing the excitement
Would never fade away.
Christmas stocking by the bed,
Apple in the toe,
Chocolate coins in golden foil,
Christmas long ago.

Pantomime and party time,
Many we remember,
Fairy lights and shiny tights,
Magic in December.
Happy smiles and caring touch,
Love which seemed to grow,
Safely stored within our hearts,
Christmas long ago.

Iris Hesselden.

Saturday — December 26

MOST of us will be familiar with the children's story "The Secret Garden" by Frances Hodgson Burnett, in which Mary and Colin restore a walled garden and their family's happiness.

Years before that book was written, the author was at a low point in her life and took refuge in her new home, Maytham Hall, where she spent countless days working in an enclosed garden. The more time she spent there, the more revitalised she felt.

Most of us don't have the luxury of a walled garden, but we can all find something to make more beautiful when we are feeling down. And in doing so, as Frances Hodgson Burnett showed, we can't help but cause the secret garden in our own hearts to flower again.

Sunday — **December 27**

I WONDER why," Edna mused as she skimmed through the December TV guide, "so many films, plays and even cartoons are based on 'A Christmas Carol'? But then perhaps," she added, "it's because it carries such a wonderful message."

I think Edna's right. Dickens's classic story remains a favourite because it contains a universal and everlasting truth – that we are at our happiest and most fulfilled when we are enriching the lives of our fellow men. And that's why I hope that the story of "A Christmas Carol" continues to be re-told for a long time to come – whatever form it happens to take!

Monday — **December 28**

IN the middle of all the destruction of war, instances of creativity are always cheering. During World War II, young South African Jack Penn was in London, learning from experts as he helped to carry out reconstructive surgery on victims of the Battle of Britain. Later, he also helped initiate such surgery in many other countries, improving the quality of life for untold patients. He even found time to become a noted sculptor.

"One of the secrets of life," he said, "is to make stepping stones out of stumbling blocks."

And we all know how useful stepping stones can be!

Tuesday — **December 29**

HOW many of us could be said to rejoice when we come headlong against life's difficulties? Not many, I suspect, so I hope these words from the Bible, James 1:2-4, will provide encouragement: "Consider it all joy, my brethren, when you encounter various trials, knowing that the testing of your faith produces endurance. And let endurance have its perfect result, so that you may be perfect and complete, lacking in nothing."

And that definitely sounds a goal worth the struggle.

Wednesday — **December 30**

IN the years before World War II, the Olympic gold medallist, Eric Liddell, gave service as a missionary in China. He travelled the country by cart, by bike or on foot, doing good where it was needed and spreading the work of God.

He was lucky if he saw his wife and young family for two months of the year and, as if that wasn't bad enough, the land he walked was being fought over by no fewer than four armies.

So how did this humble man mark the advent of a new year? He wrote a letter.

"So the good old year passes, rich with memories of the grace of God, which leads us confidently into another year, knowing that his grace is sufficient for every need."

Thursday — **December 31**

A WHOLE new year awaits us, Lord,
The path we all must tread,
And only you can see the way,
And just what lies ahead.
Will there be days of happiness,
With laughter, joy and fun?
Or times when sadness comes along,
And darkness hides the sun?

The new year is a challenge, Lord,
A chance to start anew,
But we need courage, strength and hope,
And love which comes from you.
Please walk beside us through the year,
And all our fears dispel,
Then, in our hearts, we'll hear your voice:
"Go forward, all is well."

Iris Hesselden.

PHOTOGRAPH LOCATIONS AND PHOTOGRAPHERS:

CALM WATERS – *Loch Leven, Lochaber, Scotland.*
EDZELL CASTLE – *Edzell, Angus, Scotland.*
IDYLLIC POLPERRO – *Polperro, Cornwall, England.*
SEEKING SHELTER – *View of Rum, Isle of Muck, Scotland.*
SPLENDID ISOLATION – *Luskentyre Beach, Isle of Harris, Scotland.*
CONTINENTAL COLOUR! – *Former Dutch Customs House, Torbole, Italy.*
PERTHSHIRE'S AUTUMN SHOW – *Loch Dunmore, Perthshire, Scotland.*
RUSHING BY – *Soldier's Leap, Killiecrankie, Scotland.*
STILL WATERS . . . – *Slioch, Wester Ross, Scotland.*
SANCTUARY WITHIN – *Fortingall Church, Perthshire, Scotland.*
A CRISP DAY – *Kinross-shire, Scotland.*

ACKNOWLEDGEMENTS:

David Askham: Fragile Beauty. **Matt Bain**: Splendid Isolation. **Ivan J. Belcher**: Idyllic Polperro. **Allan Devlin**: Vibrant Dahlias. **Maggie Ingall**: Taking A Break, Winter's Touch. **Douglas Laidlaw**: Borgund Stave Church, Norway. **Ian Neilson**: Tumbling Down, Continental Colour!, Sanctuary Within. **Oakleaf Marketing & Media Services**: A Sight For Sore Eyes. **Polly Pullar**: Sitting Pretty, Signs Of Spring, Best Of Friends, Bursting Forth, Seeking Shelter. **Phil Seale**: A Bit Of "Me" Time. **Willie Shand**: Daft About Daffs, Radiant Rhododenrons, Edzell Castle, Rushing By, A Crisp Day. **Sheila Taylor**: Home, Sweet Home, Perthshire's Autumn Show. **Paul Turner**: A Little Colour Makes A Big Difference! **Jack Watson Photography**: Still Waters . . . **A. White**: Calm Waters. **Richard Watson**: Stillness In Time.

A CRISP DAY